Keeping House.

For Mum

Thank you for making every house we lived
in across the globe feel like a home.

Love Em xx

Keeping House.

Creating Spaces for
Sanctuary and Celebration

EMMA BLOMFIELD
Illustrations by Juliet Sulejmani

Hardie Grant
BOOKS

[CONTENTS]

Introduction

We form our thoughts and feelings about
the word 'home' from our childhoods and
carry those emotions with us into the
first home we set up ourselves in early
adulthood. Creating a home gives us a sense
of belonging, connection and inclusion.
It's natural to want to have a place in the
world and a physical and psychological
connection to a space.

Whether you're setting up your first house from scratch or moving into a home with others, there are often so many questions to consider. What's my style? I don't have a lot of money – what should I spend it on? How many cushions is too many? What do I need in my kitchen? How can I be prepared for when family pop over unannounced, or when I have friends over for a dinner party?

This book answers those questions – it's your guidebook to creating the life you want in the space that you have, no matter where or what that may be. Perhaps you are navigating the world of home decorating for the first time and you're not sure where to start. You may be moving out of your parents' home and into your first place, or perhaps after years of renting you've bought your first house with a significant other and together you're traversing the tricky terrain of combining your possessions. Maybe you are living alone or moving in with a few friends, or perhaps you're renting out the spare room on Airbnb to help cover the mortgage. Whatever the situation, there's no reason why we can't all create a comfortable and inviting space to feel at home in.

What are you waiting for?

Our homes are more than just a roof over our heads and a place to store our stuff – we all deserve to find the pleasure and enjoyment that comes with decorating our sacred spaces and then sharing them with others. Yet so many of us seem to put it off.

Do you hear yourself coming up with any of these excuses?

+ But I'm just renting.
+ But I'm living in my parents' house.
+ But this old hand-me-down furniture isn't that bad, is it?
+ But I'm so busy at the moment – I'll get around to decorating next week, or next month, or maybe next year …
+ But I'm waiting until I meet the right person – then we'll create a home together.
+ But I don't intend on being here for long.

+ But it will probably cost too much to decorate or entertain the way I want to.
+ But I can't have people over for dinner – I don't have anywhere for them to sit …
+ But I've got no taste.
+ But I don't really know where to start.

Yes, some of these are very valid reasons not to go out and spend a fortune on new furniture, especially if you intend on moving soon. But there is one very obvious theme here that needs to be challenged: 'I'm waiting for …'

So, dear reader, what *are* you waiting for? Ditch the 'one day' mentality and start living in the present.

I challenge you to start thinking in a different way.

+ You can make simple changes to your existing space to make it feel more 'you', no matter what your home situation is.
+ It doesn't have to cost the earth.
+ Absolutely everyone can decorate a great room and throw a great party.

If you can alter your approach, you'll realise this is your shot to start creating and working towards your 'one day'. Life is constantly evolving and changing for everyone, but living in the moment allows you to be more engaged in your life. You'll be more invested in turning your house into a home and having your friends and family over to enjoy it with you, and you'll find you're happier in your home because of the effort you've put into it. You don't need to wait until you are in your forever home to create your own haven, and you don't need to wait until everything is perfectly in place before you invite people over. You *can* achieve a meaningful home regardless of the situation you find yourself in.

It's normal to feel overwhelmed.

More often than not, the reason we don't start a project is because we don't know where to start. It's a pretty intimidating task when you think about it: fitting out an entire space to be a true reflection of your style and taste, showing off your decorating skills, and selecting practical pieces that will serve you and the other occupants of the home well. We all want to create a welcoming space for guests yet at the same time we worry they'll pass judgement on our decorating choices, or the food and drinks we serve. In the search for perfection we end up in a complete state of overwhelm, analysing every single detail but not actually making any decisions. It's a vicious cycle!

It doesn't help that the perfectly styled images of Pinterest and Instagram can often lead to feelings of inadequacy. Comparing your reality with these images isn't beneficial. Yes, they are great for inspiration, but don't get caught up in trying to re-create the entire look or you'll lose sight of the goal: to create a home or host a gathering that is a reflection of *you*. Often these images are carefully crafted just for the camera; they don't actually make very practical places to live. This is partly why this book is illustrated – it takes the pressure off replicating exact looks and forces you to use your own creativity. We all have it; we just need to tap into it.

You may experience a range of emotions throughout the decorating or entertaining process, from pure frustration and despair through to utter joy and happiness when you get it right. Stick with the journey. This book will hopefully help keep you sane and get you to the final destination: ultimate home love!

'Don't lose sight of the goal: to create a home or host a gathering that is a reflection of *you*.'

HOW TO USE THIS BOOK

I have divided this book into two parts. Part I, Sanctuary, covers all the essentials for setting up and decorating your home. We jump right into how your home is the truest reflection of you, your travels and what inspires you, and how to collate those ideas in your space. Part II, Celebration, explores the art of creating a space to share with the people we love.

Each part opens with some basics to help you get your head around the fundamentals of decorating and entertaining. Then, throughout the following chapters, I'll cover concepts like finishing touches, or when to save and when to splurge. And along the way you'll get my little tips on how to bring everything together.

These days, whenever we've got a question or query, we tend to turn to our trusty pal Google for the answer. I'd like to challenge this and kick it old-school. I am an avid reader and a visual learner so I tend to turn to books, rather than digital formats, for advice when it comes to decorating and entertaining. Let this be your well-worn, handy how-to manual to guide you through all manner of domestic chaos and decorating dilemmas, from how many knives you need to set the table for a formal occasion, what thread count your sheets need to be, and how to personalise your new rental and still get your bond back, to things you can do to boost your confidence when entertaining, and how to throw an epic grown-up dinner party (without upsetting the neighbours).

Tip

Your home is the greatest reflection of yourself – surround yourself with beauty.

Sanctuary

Your home is
a bit like your
wardrobe in a way;
it's an expression
of your style.

As a child I was fortunate enough to live overseas for several years. Each time we moved to a new country I would watch Mum and Dad set up the entire house for us. Although my two younger brothers and I would moan about being dragged around furniture stores for hours on end, we had to admit that it was exciting to have a completely new bedroom every few years. Within the first weeks of arriving in a new country, Mum would start by buying all the basics and then, over time, she would add personality to the home with artwork and other beautiful cultural pieces that we collected on our weekend trips.

In my final year of schooling, my family moved to Hong Kong and I moved into the boarding house at my school back home in Sydney so that my studies wouldn't be too disrupted. I wasn't particularly happy about it, but Mum made every effort to make the transition as seamless as possible. We went shopping for things for my new shoebox-sized bedroom – a doona cover with matching pillows, a stereo system that matched the colour of the doona (cringe!) and a few posters to hang on the walls – and then I was left to set up the room and make it feel homely. Thankfully I'd had years of watching Mum do this, so I had a bit of an idea about where to start.

Shelter is one of our most basic needs in life and being accepted and understood in our environment goes hand in hand. Your home doesn't need to win you any awards or be photographed for a design magazine, but it does need to be a place where you can relax and be yourself, where you can entertain friends, and retreat to at the end of a busy day with a glass of wine and a good book. This section is all about crafting and creating your own sanctuary, from setting up the basics to the things you can do to make your house feel like a home.

DIFY – DO IT FOR YOURSELF

Keep in mind that you are decorating *your* home for *you*. If you can't be honest with yourself about your style, you'll always feel like a guest in your own home. Don't decorate for the sake of being on trend or because you want to impress your guests. It's fine to create a space for friends to enjoy too, but that shouldn't be your driving factor. Think about how you want to feel when you come home each day and how your home supports you. If you're feeling burnt out at work, coming home to a cosy space where you can relax and unwind is the perfect cure. You're decorating for your own happiness and your home is an extension of you – so what do you want it to say about you?

Five steps towards creating an authentic home

+ Own your style wholeheartedly! It's hard not to be swept up in buying items for your home because you think that's what you should have, or what everyone says you should have. It's important that you remain true to yourself. If you love it, then buy it. If you don't love it, toss it.
+ Don't take decorating too seriously; we can't live in a magazine photo shoot all the time.
+ Embrace the imperfections; it's what gives your home authenticity and character.
+ Don't underestimate the power and personality that a quirky piece of furniture or trinket bought while on holidays can bring to the room.
+ Accessorise with what you've got lying around. You don't need a big budget to create a home that is a true reflection of you.

Creating an authentic home is a journey of self-discovery too. You'll learn all sorts of things about yourself and the way you prefer to live while on the decorating journey. If you're on the journey with a significant other, you'll both be learning these lessons together – hopefully in harmony!

WHERE DO I START?

Before you can start to think about decorating your space, you need to assess how the space is working and what you'd like to change. Once you've got a clear idea in your head, you will find it easier to edit the things you have, make decisions about what you need and start to style your space.

Step 1
Assess

Walk through your home and view it as a visitor. Pretend you are inspecting it as a potential buyer. Look closely at the architecture – walls, doors, windows and ceiling height – and write a list of anything that bothers you. Do the doorways dictate a certain traffic flow through the room? Are the windows low to the ground so furniture will block the light when placed in front of them? Do you have low ceilings that make you feel boxed in? As you go through each room, take note of some of the less tangible things as well. Is there enough natural light in the room? Is the house always a few degrees too warm or cool? Is there a musty smell you notice in winter time? You may be able to find solutions to some of these problems during the decorating process, but some things will need to be dealt with down the track. Put the list on the fridge and tick the items off as you deal with them.

Assess the pieces you already own. Can you move any items from other rooms to jazz up the living room? Could you reframe artwork from another room and move it into the bedroom? Search through cupboards, drawers, forgotten boxes and storage areas such as the garage. 'Shopping' at home saves you having to spend more of your hard-earned cash – and you never know what forgotten treasures you may find stashed away. Make a list of your ideas or put the items together in a box or cupboard.

Step 2
Edit

Ask yourself if you truly need/want/love the items you own. If it's a no, chuck it. If it has no functional purpose and it doesn't bring you joy, toss it out. Be ruthless! There's no point hanging onto things with negative emotions attached to them, so remove anything that doesn't serve a purpose or bring you joy to look at.

Don't attempt this for the entire house in one hit. To stop you from becoming overwhelmed, break the task into rooms and then into categories (such as furniture, soft furnishings, art and decorative items). Anything that no longer serves you can be recycled or given away.

On the other hand, don't feel as though you have to get rid of everything. You'll always find treasures on your travels that you'll want to bring home and incorporate into your decor. Don't deny yourself these little trinkets, because these items personalise your space; they start to build a story about you.

Step 3
Style

Now you can start to style the space based on what you felt needed to change. If traffic flow is an issue, think about moving the furniture around. If your ceilings feel low, consider hanging your window treatments as high as possible to add a sense of height. If the room feels cold and lacking in personality, perhaps add a thick woollen statement rug. Play around with the placement of your existing pieces – items you've had sitting in the study could find a new lease of life in the living room, or vice versa. The following chapters will give you plenty to think about when it comes to style.

A word on
mindset

Check in while you're doing the 'assess, edit, style' task
to see if you have a negative or positive mindset towards
your home – you may be surprised to find you feel quite
pessimistic about certain elements. Watch that this
doesn't continue throughout the decorating process.
Try to reframe your thoughts into more positive ones
about what your home means to you: comfort, safety,
security, a loving space for you and your family and
friends. Decorative elements can be added to reinforce
positive feelings, so keep persisting with the book and
you'll be totally in love with your home by the end.

HOME AND THE FIVE SENSES

As you progress through the decorating process, keep in mind the five human senses and their impact on the memories we make at home. Does your environment support your five senses in a positive way?

Sight

Sight is usually the first sense that comes into play as soon as you enter a room, so you want it to be a pleasant experience for your eyeballs.

+ Clear the clutter. Your home will be a lot more visually appealing if it's tidy.
+ Lighting is a huge contributor here, as it can make or break the mood of the room. Soft lighting helps enhance the atmosphere in the evenings, whereas task lighting is important if it's above your desk or kitchen bench.
+ Colours and patterns play a significant role, too. Vibrant colours can excite the mind, so think about the sort of vibe you want to create in this space: calm and tranquil or loud and fun?

Touch

Tactile textures stimulate a sense of touch, and in your home you want this to be a pleasant experience. Strong feelings are often triggered by touch. Is your sofa fabric scratchy? You'll be jumping off in no time. Are the dining chairs too hard on your back? You won't be spending much time there either. Create a happy home by carefully selecting the materials you use.

+ Think about different textures for different seasons – wool for winter, cotton for summer.
+ The materials you choose for your bath towels, throw rugs and bed linen should be the best quality you can afford, as they come into direct contact with your skin. Don't compromise here, even if it looks fabulous, because you'll regret it every time you have a shower or hop into bed.

+ Similarly, take care when choosing carpets, floorboard finishes, sofa fabrics, dining chairs and bedhead upholstery – these are items that you are walking on or touching every day.

+ Add a little touch of luxury here and there to make each room feel special. Perhaps look for some luxe faux-fur cushions and a super-soft throw rug for your sofa. These textures can also make the space feel cosy and inviting.

+ Timber furniture pieces, especially those with rustic finishes, add warmth to a room and connect your home to nature.

+ Varying the textures in your home makes the journey through each room all the more pleasing, as each room reveals different elements to look at, discover and play with.

+ If your guests are wandering through your home picking up and touching things as they go, take it as a compliment that they like what you've picked out rather than scolding them for messing up your perfectly placed cushions or ornaments.

Tip

Layering different textures in a room can have just as much impact on a space as bold colours: for example, a woollen rug on floorboards, complemented by a raw linen sofa dressed with a variety of scatter cushions.

Sound

Just as certain songs can trigger strong emotions and memories, the little creaks and noises you hear around your home can greatly affect your mood, in both negative and positive ways.

+ Appliances that ding or buzz all day can negatively affect your emotions, so look for alternatives or ways to switch them off.
+ Placing rugs on hard surfaces, such as tiled floors or creaky hallways, can help muffle unwanted sounds and absorb some of the echo in a large space.
+ Background music helps to create an atmosphere and can lift your mood.
+ The sound of a crackling fire or a flickering candle can add to the relaxed feeling of your home and shouldn't be overlooked in the decorating process.

Taste

Appealing to the sense of taste may seem difficult when it comes to decorating – hopefully you aren't actually licking the walls and furniture – but there are many ways we can stimulate this sense, particularly in the kitchen and dining room.

+ A bowl of lemons or mangoes on the kitchen bench not only adds a pop of colour but serves to remind you of your sense of taste.
+ Take colour into consideration. Red is thought to stimulate the appetite, so think about including some red in your dining room decor.
+ Also consider where food and drink will be placed when you're not sitting at the dining table. Do you have adequate side tables or space on the coffee table to put your glass of wine or cup of tea?
+ Place a pretty plate of mints or a small glass bowl filled with wrapped chocolates on your hall table. These will appeal to both the sense of taste and sight.

Smell

The sense of smell is linked very closely to memory and can create positive or negative emotions. The aroma of coffee beans roasting, the smell of gardenias wafting in from the garden, scented candles burning softly in the evenings or the musty smell of old books on your bookshelf can all trigger happy memories.

Why not think about creating your own signature scent for your home? An easy way to do this is to play around with scented candles, room sprays, essential-oil burners and reed diffuser sticks until you find something that works for you. Experiment with using different scents in different rooms.

- **+ Entryway:** Choose a welcoming scent for your guests to enjoy as they walk in the front door. Some options include verbena, lemongrass and rosemary.
- **+ Living room:** You don't always want to feel too relaxed and dozy in your living space, so use fresh, crisp or woody scents such as sandalwood, fig, bergamot, amber, gardenia, rose, orange blossom or jasmine.
- **+ Dining room:** It's best to avoid overly sweet smells in the dining room, such as strawberry, vanilla and coconut, as these will affect your experience while eating. For this room, stick to fresh scents such as geranium, patchouli or spruce.
- **+ Kitchen:** This is tricky because you don't want your scented candles or sprays to overpower the aroma of your beautiful cooking. Try fresh green scents such as basil, cucumber, moss, grapefruit or currant.
- **+ Bedroom:** Lavender promotes sleep, so use an essential-oil diffuser or rub the oil on the soles of your feet to aid slumber. Other scents for relaxation include lily, jasmine and rose.
- **+ Study:** Some work-enhancing scents for the home office include peppermint, lemon and bergamot.
- **+ Bathroom:** Opt for a crisp, clean scent for the bathroom to counteract any nasty smells. Citrus scents such as lime, lemon or mandarin, or the fresh smell of eucalyptus, are excellent choices.

Sanctuary

Colour my world

Choosing colours for your home can be confusing. Do you extend the same palette throughout the whole house, or can you vary the colours for different rooms? You need to consider the house as a whole, especially when it comes to open-plan spaces, but you don't need to follow a strict colour palette in every room or you'll tire of it much faster. Carry one or two colours through to the next room – a neutral colour works well in this instance, or navy or black.

Colours can also be very overwhelming when you first open a fabric or paint swatch book. The tiny swatch before you is not enough to decide whether a certain fabric will look great on your chair or cushions, or if that grey paint will look too dark when it's on the wall in your living room. And never buy fabric or paint based on how you *think* it might look in your home. When looking at fabric swatches, always ask the store for a cutting so you can see it in various lights at home, as well as against other things such as your flooring, wall paint and furniture. When choosing paint, it's best to purchase a sample pot of paint and experiment on the walls first. Paint a few patches on different walls in the room, so you can see how the colour looks as the light changes throughout the day.

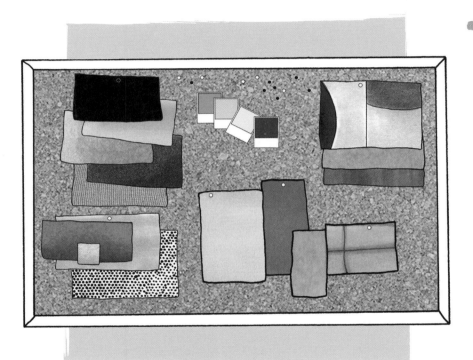

MIXING AND MATCHING

While styling your home, think about whether you would prefer a more casual or formal look. Casual furniture is typically more relaxed looking – think slipcovers, deep seats, loose covers and linen that crinkles – and generally the colours are monochromatic or neutral with little or no pattern. Formal furniture features more structured upholstery with buttons and studs, timber surrounds and frames, upright backs and antique pieces. Formal pieces are generally fussier in their designs with ornate detailing, smaller floral patterns and heavier weighted fabrics – think back to your grandparents' front room, also known as the 'good room'. The architecture of your home is something to consider here: Victorian or Art Deco homes and units can pull off formal furniture due to their ornate architectural details, whereas modern, seaside or country homes often suit a more casual vibe.

But don't think you have to choose one style over another if you don't want to – you could include a mix of both styles, or go for a predominantly relaxed feel and add a few formal hero pieces here and there. You don't want to look like you went to one furniture store and bought everything in one hit (although no judgement if that's all you had the patience for that day) – you want your rooms to tell an interesting story upon walking in.

Which wood?

The question of 'mix or match' applies for timber furnishings, too. So that you don't give your room an overly flat and 'matchy-matchy' feel, avoid matching all the timbers in the room to the same hue. But how do you work out what coloured timbers go together? Mixing the timber stains at the opposite ends of the colour spectrum is the easiest way to work this out. For example, if you have a coffee table in a dark chocolate colour and want to work a timber dining table into the room as well, then opt for a lighter toned timber for the dining table. Likewise, if you've got dark-stained floors, a dining table in a lighter wood will give the room a more balanced look. When in doubt, woods painted in white or black are easily worked into most timber colour schemes.

Tip

If you've got a timber table on timber floorboards, place a rug underneath the table so that the timbers aren't in direct contact with each other.

Conscious
acquisition

From here on out let's start thinking longer term when buying items, big or small, for your home. Just because you've done a clear out and have more space doesn't mean you need to fill it immediately. Don't buy things on impulse or items you intend to replace in a year or less. Make the conscious decision to acquire less, make better choices when it comes to adding to your home, and be aware of the impact your purchases have on the environment.

Nowadays so many homewares and pieces of furniture end up in landfill. This is in stark contrast to our grandparents' generation when things were made to last, when they held onto the same armchair or table for decades and just re-covered them or repaired them when they needed to. Let's bring that mentality into the twenty-first century and stop the instant gratification and mega consumption levels we've somehow grown used to in the last few decades.

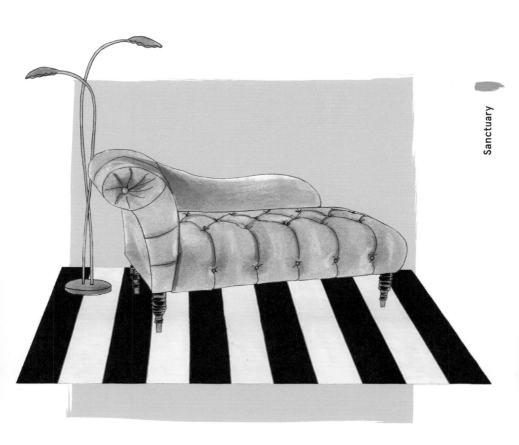

LET'S GO SHOPPING

Once you've got a clear idea of what you need for your space, it's time to hit the shops. Before you head out, it's important to make a list of what you're looking for to avoid making rash decisions later on.

Purchasing panic

Even if you'd made a list, purchase decisions can be fraught with anxiety. To help you see things more clearly and to prevent panic buying when you're shopping, ask yourself the following questions:

+ Does the item serve my home practically or is it just a pretty thing that doesn't actually have a purpose?
+ Is it in proportion to the rest of the room? Will it sit comfortably between the two windows in the living room or against the wall?
+ Does it work with the other items I already own (and which I don't plan on changing any time soon)?
+ Can I see this in my home in ten or more years? Or will it look dated after a year or so?
+ Will I lose sleep over this if I don't buy it?
+ Do I need this item now or can I go away and think about it?

Sanctuary

Tip

Shopping centre lighting can dramatically impact the true colour of items, so check the store's return policy before committing in case something doesn't look quite right at home.

Splurge versus save

We have so many choices these days in terms of quality, but being realistic about what you should and shouldn't be investing in will help keep your budget on track. Break your shopping list down into the essential items and what you can afford to buy up front. You will find that your design and overall style will start to evolve after the first few big purchases, and then you can bring it all together with stages two and three. As a rough guide, you should allocate about 60 per cent of your budget to stage one, and then divide the remaining 40 per cent between stages two and three.

Stage 1
Big-ticket items

It's worthwhile allocating more of your budget to grounding pieces such as your dining table, sofa and bed. You use these every day, and buying quality once will serve you for years to come rather than buying inferior quality over and over.

Stage 2
Secondary furniture items

Side tables, lamps, console tables, hall tables, sideboards, bookshelves and cabinets – these smaller elements of the room are functional yet decorative. They provide visual balance for the big-ticket items.

Stage 3
Finishing touches

These things aren't as important on a day-to-day basis, but they are necessary nonetheless. They act as fun accents and kick up the energy in the room while also tying together the colour scheme. Finishing touches include plants, cushions, rugs, mirrors, curtains, artwork and decor items. Save your money on these, as you may want to update them as trends come and go.

The
waiting game

Don't expect to be able to walk into a new space and instantly know how it should all come together. Good homes take time to evolve. Putting too much pressure on yourself to get it all done within a certain time frame is stressful and takes away from the decorating process, which should be enjoyable. You'll find yourself making rushed decisions when buying furniture or other things for your home and regretting them later; you never know when you may stumble upon the perfect chair to complete your room. And it's totally fine to ignore things that require a larger budget to tackle – the time for those things will come. Have patience and accept that things will change along the way.

You may never truly feel done with decorating; there will always be something you want to change or add to a room, and that's perfectly okay. It's part of the journey of decorating.

FINDING FOCUS

What do you notice when you first walk into a room? Is it a beautiful painting or a fireplace, or is it something that catches your eye for all the wrong reasons? When decorating, it's important that you create a focal point for each room. It gives the eye somewhere to rest when you first walk in, rather than darting here and there because the room is too cluttered.

Sanctuary

+ In most rooms the focal point will be somewhere on the wall, so hanging a striking artwork or gallery of artwork will ensure your eyes rest there when you enter the room (see pages 92–3 for tips on hanging art).
+ If you're lucky enough to have a beautiful fireplace with a mantelshelf above it, this automatically becomes the room's focal point, and you can style around it to make the most of it.
+ Alternatively, use a buffet or entry hall console as your focal point by styling a lovely vignette on the tabletop and hanging a round mirror above to bounce some additional light into the room.
+ Focal points don't always need to be big colourful pieces. You can create a textural focal point by incorporating different materials into the room (see pages 24–5 for some ideas on textures in your home).
+ If you're feeling bold, use your sofa or bedhead as the focal point in your living room or bedroom. Opt for a fun fabric to really draw attention to it, but ensure you keep the other elements textural or plain so as not to detract from the focal point.
+ If your room doesn't have any striking features, you could paint one wall a feature colour or perhaps bring in some large statement pot plants.

Tip

Sometimes a room's focal point is not what you want it to be, so tricking the eye to focus elsewhere can help mask the big TV or the view of the neighbour's old wooden fence out the window.

FINISHING TOUCHES

Have you ever walked into a room and thought that it just didn't feel quite right? It's most likely because the finishing touches weren't there yet. You might have all your big-ticket pieces of furniture in place, but it's the final details – art, rugs, mirrors, stylish ornaments, scatter cushions and lamps – that can really make the room look fabulous.

But how do you get all your decorating decor to work together? The easiest way is to pick a colour or texture and repeat this common element throughout the finishing touches. For example, if your artwork features navy blue, then ensure you have elements of navy in your rug, in the pattern on your scatter cushions and perhaps the lampshade as well. That one element will keep it cohesive and help tie the room together.

Tip

Adding some life to the room with fresh flowers or a potted plant (faux or real) goes a long way to finishing off the room.

What is a vignette?

Not to be mistaken for the word 'vinaigrette', a vignette is a grouping of ornaments or things in one place to form a little scene or tell a story (and most definitely not a dressing for your salad leaves). At Christmas time we often style certain areas of the home to depict little Christmas scenes, but there's no reason why you can't create vignettes all year round. Changing your vignette can have a great impact on the room as a whole and means you aren't spending a fortune to redecorate. They're also a good talking point for your guests, especially if you're showing off special trinkets found on your travels or found objects from a bushwalk in the country.

You can create a vignette on any flat surface – try the coffee table, bedside table, sideboard in the dining room, or entry table by the front door.

Some tips for styling your vignette

+ Varying the shapes, sizes and height of the items is key to getting the look right. Start with a taller item, like a narrow vase filled with a cluster of lovely flowers, then add a short, squat item such as a crystal paper weight to contrast the tall vase.
+ Using trays is the key to a well-styled vignette as it keeps all the items housed neatly together.
+ Give the items some room to breathe; don't cram them all together as it won't be as visually pleasing.
+ A stack of books helps give some stepped definition to the display.
+ Add a candle in an interesting jar for some colour and fun.
+ Work in groupings in odd numbers – think a stack of three books instead of four, or one candle instead of two.
+ If you're stuck for ideas about how to style and theme your vignette, think about the seasons, colours or design themes (like Scandinavian or coastal) to spark your inspiration.

The 'shelfie'

If you don't have a lot of room to start creating vignettes all over your house, then try the 'shelfie'. Clear out one shelf in your bookshelf and create your own shelfie to show off your styling skills. Use a mix of books, ornaments, vases, candles, bookends and found objects to tell your story. It will not only add interest to the room but also help to break up the solid wall of books.

The whole point of creating shelfies or other vignettes is to experiment with your creativity, so keep playing around until you feel it all works well together. Taking a photo of your handiwork can help identify any areas that need filling in, as seeing it in 2D form will highlight these gaps.

Personalisation on a budget

Not everyone has a huge pool of cash to pour into decorating. Of course when your surroundings are more luxurious it feels better, but ultimately we want to feel safe, secure, warm and comfortable in our homes, and having a small budget shouldn't jeopardise that.

One trick is to combine high- and low-value pieces to create a meaningful space. Buy a few quality pieces that you love and mix them with a few things you know you'll eventually need to replace – that's okay, as long as they serve a good purpose in the interim. Don't rush out to buy quality pieces all at once – you will find them when the time is right.

It's important to remain realistic throughout the process. Sometimes you'll find that no matter how many times you scrub the linoleum floor in the kitchen you still won't have a show home, and that's completely fine – you can still make the space a home. The key is to make a feature or focal point elsewhere. Distract from the eyesore by covering it up or deflecting attention elsewhere: throw down a rug to disguise ugly flooring or hang a bold piece of art to act as the feature in a room.

Use what you've already got, to find a sense of satisfaction from repurposing or redefining how an item is used in your home. This will save you money and sharpen your creative skills. Use sites like Pinterest for inspiration and then go shopping in your own home to find a way to pull together some new looks.

A few ideas to consider

+ Take out that glass vase of your grandmother's that you had sitting in a box and use it. Add some fresh flowers and display it on the table in the entryway.
+ Light the candle you've been saving. What are you saving it for? Dusty candles are never a good look no matter how expensive they were.
+ Change out the photos in your frames for more recent ones.

+ Instead of keeping them hidden in a drawer, tack your polaroids from a friend's wedding up around a mirror and leave it messy and abstract – your home should reflect your life and personality.
+ Use the little tissue box cover your aunt gave you for your birthday. Making a boring cardboard box nicer to look at means you can happily keep it on display.
+ If sharing the house with friends or a significant other, it's important that each person is represented in the room. Perhaps corral meaningful mementoes from each person on a wooden tray and display it on your coffee or hall table.

When to call in professional help

Some people seem to have an innate ability to throw different elements in a room and bring it all together, while others struggle significantly. It is more than okay to admit you're in over your head once you start on your decorating journey. Even experienced decorators can sometimes feel stumped by certain projects and need to refer to all sorts of resources to find a design solution. If the funds allow and you know you need some professional help, where do you start to look? Firstly, you need to work out if your project needs a designer or a decorator, but who does what? They sound familiar, but they actually perform different tasks.

Decorator

A decorator, or stylist, specialises in aesthetics and will specify soft furnishings, furniture and decorative items for your home. Usually a decorator will enter the project after the building work is complete to commence the furniture-buying process; they have extensive knowledge of fabrics, the use of colour and furniture suppliers. A decorator works with you to incorporate your personality and character into your home. It varies in different countries, but typically a decorator or stylist does not need to have studied interior design to work in that role.

Designer

A designer is involved in a project from the planning and building stage, and can even work with your architect to make design decisions regarding fixed features such as flooring, benchtops and hardware. A designer's main role is to focus on function and spatial planning, but they will also specify lighting fixtures and work with the builder to wire the home accordingly. To be qualified to work as a designer usually requires university study.

Working with a designer or decorator

Prior to meeting with your decorator or designer, do your homework: flip through some magazines, scroll through your pins on Pinterest, and make a list of any questions you have. When meeting with your designer, show them the inspirational images you have collected; this is a brilliant way to visually relay your style and taste, and what you hope to achieve. The more specific you can be, the better the outcome.

The process after the initial meeting will vary from designer to designer, but you can expect that it will be similar to the following:

+ **Initial consultation:** Your designer meets with you in your home to assess each room you'd like help with and decipher your style and tastes.
+ **Design plan:** Your designer then goes away and works on a mood board or design action plan, complete with furniture and decor suggestions to suit your space.
+ **Design process:** After reviewing your designer's suggestions or tweaking certain elements, the ordering may begin.
+ **Completion:** After the furniture has been ordered and delivered, your designer may visit again to style the rooms and add any finishing touches to the space.

How long is the whole process?

Each project is unique, so the process may take anywhere from three weeks up to a year, or even more for some projects. Custom furniture can take four to twelve weeks (or more!) to be made, and if the furniture is shipped from overseas the designer is at the mercy of customs and shipping constraints. Sometimes your tradespeople will get held up unexpectedly when they start ripping walls down or removing floors, the painter might take longer to paint, or the flooring company might take longer to install carpet than initially quoted.

Trying to place strict deadlines on the decorating process is fruitless; there will always be unforeseen delays here and there that can't be helped. Rushing this process can end in mistakes, so often the extra time can help you get used to the new changes taking place, or give you time to tweak your overall decorating plan as the project evolves.

Live

Live

We call this room several different names – lounge room, family room or sitting room – but living room is probably the most accurate description, as it truly is a room for living in. We do so much more than lounge around in a living room: we entertain guests, watch Netflix, host cheese nights, play board games on the coffee table, dance around the furniture while playing Singstar, or console a friend on the sofa with a glass of wine after another bad date. See, a lot of living happens in this room!

SPLURGE VERSUS SAVE

It's probably fairly obvious what we need to splurge on when buying furniture for the living room, but maybe you're not so sure where you can save money. Here's a handy guide for setting up the living room.

Stage 1
Big-ticket items

A sofa, TV unit and coffee table are your top priority purchases and should be locked down before anything else. These three purchases are your most expensive items – they'll be used the most and hopefully should last you through many moves. If your sofa has good bones and is good quality, it can always be re-covered down the line.

Stage 2
Secondary items

Once your big-ticket items are sorted, think about adding side tables, table lamps, floor lamps and armchairs. Spend a bit less on these.

Stage 3
Finishing touches

Rugs, art and scatter cushions for the sofa are really important to finish off the room and help tie together your overall colour palette. Pick up colours from your rug or art when choosing cushions.

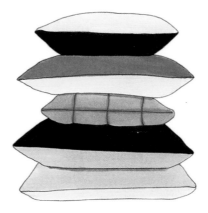

A WORD ON SIZE AND PROPORTIONS

This is *the* most important element in decorating to get right, especially when it comes to your living room. Taking the time to measure all your purchases prior to adding them to your space will stop you from making expensive mistakes. Just because a massive L-shaped modular lounge will fit across the length of your living room wall doesn't always mean it's the right choice proportionally. Take the other walls and furniture items into consideration.

Often your TV placement will dictate where the rest of your furniture sits, so get this right up front and your sofa, coffee table, rug and side table placement will come together naturally. Adding one or two floor lamps to the corners of the room will help balance out the longer horizontal pieces and add some height to the space.

You also need to consider the size of your doorways, or the elevator if you're living in an apartment. Will your new furniture fit through them? You don't want to be stuck with a three-seater sofa that doesn't fit in the elevator or a sideboard that's too big to go up the stairs to your home, so measure the size of the relevant doorways *before* you go shopping. If the items are too large, are there other ways around the problem? Can you use rope to haul the sofa in over the balcony railing? Are the legs on the sofa or sideboard removable? Often it's only the legs that stop you from getting the piece down the hallway.

Tip

If there is a TV unit opposite your sofa, the sofa should be about 40–50 cm (16–20 in) wider than the TV unit on each side. If the TV unit is longer than your sofa, your entire room will feel off kilter.

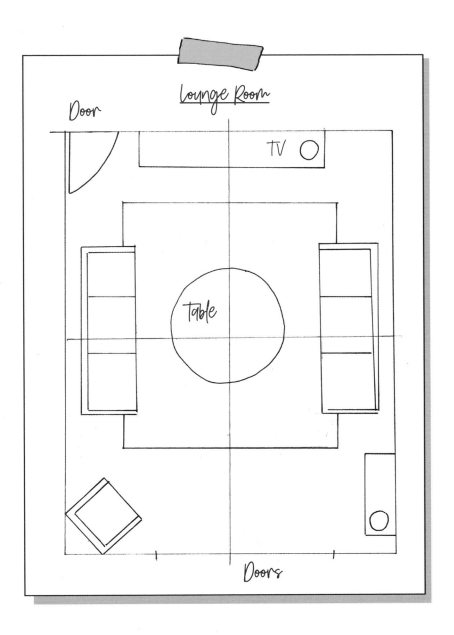

Lounge Room

Door

TV

Table

Doors

Ottomans versus
coffee tables

Ottoman or coffee table? It's a common debate when deciding on living room furniture. Ottomans make for comfy footrests but aren't practical if you want to pop a cup of tea on top of them. Placing a tray on the ottoman will help keep the items stable, but a coffee table is a much sturdier choice if you want somewhere to rest your legs *and* keep plates of food or glasses of wine stable.

LIGHTING

Lighting is often overlooked in many homes, but plays one of the most important roles in decorating. Lighting adds atmosphere – light and bright or soft and moody – and style and texture to your room. It can be pretty as well as practical, so why not have some fun with it?

Assigning a specific purpose to lighting in your living space will help you work out exactly what you need.

For mood or ambient lighting

+ **Lamps:** These are great for mood lighting at night. To create an ambient mood in the evening, turn off all the bright downlights and switch on the floor and table lamps. Your lampshades can tie into the colour scheme of the room, while the lamp bases dictate the overall style and design of the space.
+ **Wall sconces:** Wash your walls with a soft yellow light by installing some sconces. A pair of sconces either side of a buffet table frames the wall nicely.
+ **Candles:** Don't underestimate the power of candles. Not only do they provide a nice warm glow when lit but also scent your living space beautifully.

Task lighting for when you really need to see what you're doing

+ **Desk lamps:** These are usually shorter than the lamps in the living room, as they are specifically for task lighting. Anglepoise lamps are a good choice, as you can direct the light down onto your desk or work area.
+ **Pendants:** Hang pendant lights above the coffee table to light your living space, or above your kitchen island for extra lighting when cooking. Be careful not to hang pendant lights too low so that they obstruct your view through the room or are a hazard to the tall.
+ **Track lighting:** These are usually installed on the ceiling or a wall. The advantage of this type of lighting is that the individual lights can be repositioned to direct light wherever it's needed.
+ **Under-shelf lighting:** These are mostly seen in the kitchen, often installed under cupboards, but they can also be used to add extra lighting for a work space.

Tip

Play around with lampshades to change up the look of your living room. If you have a plain lamp base, use a fun patterned print for the shade.

Sanctuary — *Live*

When you want to make a design statement

+ **Statement pendants:** These are centred to the room for maximum impact. If you have high ceilings, they can make a fabulous focal point in the room.
+ **Sculptural floor lamps:** If adding or changing the existing overhead lighting is not an option, use statement floor lamps to light up a dark corner in the evening. These sit pretty during the day when not in use, and can easily move with you from home to home.

Know
your glow

When selecting light bulbs for the living room, opt for a yellow (or warm white) light bulb rather than a crisp white one. Yellow bulbs are more flattering to the skin and aren't as harsh, so add to the overall atmosphere in the room. Cool white bulbs light the room in the same way a hospital room is often lit, so are best used in areas such as the kitchen or study.

STORAGE

It's often difficult to decide whether to go for built-in or freestanding storage. Built-in cupboards and bookshelves are an excellent investment as you'll see that money back when selling your home, but if you're a renter or planning to move soon, then freestanding storage will be your best friend.

Bookshelves with a combination of closed and open shelves allow greater flexibility for your storage needs. You can neatly display some items on the shelves and keep the less attractive items hidden behind closed doors – plus it means there's less shelves to dust.

Cabinets, buffets and sideboards are also great pieces for the living room. That then gives you the perfect spot for your new lamp, plus you've got an empty flat surface to show off your styling skills.

Don't forget your TV unit also doubles as a freestanding storage unit. You could consider using a taller unit like a buffet and then mount your TV on the wall above it to get the most out of the furniture piece.

Likewise, coffee tables with a shelf underneath for storage are perfect for keeping magazines, remote controls and other bits and bobs tidy rather than messing up the top of the table. If your table doesn't have a shelf, think about putting a cane basket or wooden box under the table to store extra throw rugs or reading material. Keep small items such as the TV remote controls tidy by storing them in wooden or decorative trays.

Tip

Just because the storage is there and available doesn't mean you need to fill it. A biannual assessment of what you've got hidden away in your storage units will help keep clutter under control.

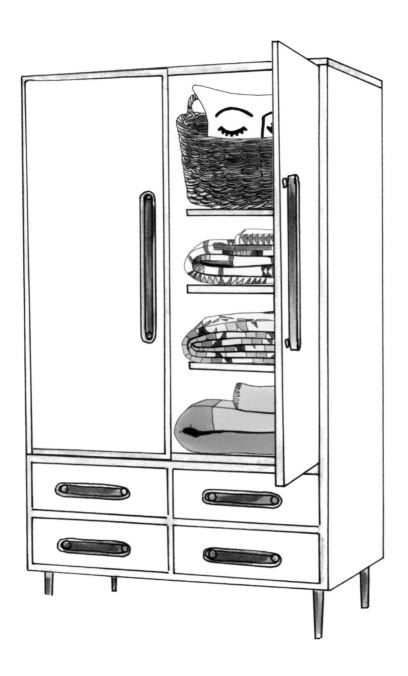

Outdoor
living

When the weather warms up the first thing we want to do is fling open the doors and sit outside in the beautiful sunshine with a glass of wine. We spend a lot of time outdoors in summer, so why not set up an outdoor area in your own home?

Before you start planning the space and what you'll need, you will have to decide how you want to use it. Do you have outdoor space for an eating area as well as a lounging area, or is it just one or the other? Which do you think you'd benefit from most: a spot to sit and relax with a book, or a little cafe table to have breakfast at?

The next factor to consider is the weather. Will the furniture be exposed to the elements or is the area under cover? If the furniture is exposed to the elements, you might be wise to spend a little more for quality items if the budget allows.

If you only have a small outdoor area to work with, such as a balcony or courtyard, you can still make it homely. An outdoor or waterproof rug will give the furniture an anchor point, plus they're super easy to clean – just turn on the hose and wash off any food scraps, leaves or grime. Bring some character to the space by adding some scatter cushions to your seating, but bring them inside when they're not in use or opt for outdoor fabric covers with weatherproof and mould-resistant inserts.

Don't forget to light your outdoor area. You'll want to enjoy the space from afternoon dappled light through to late into the evening, so artificial lighting is a must. If your balcony is covered, wall-mounted sconces are great lighting choices, as are overhead pendant lights, which are both decorative and functional. Candles also add to the ambience but the flickering light can attract bugs, so a few battery-operated flameless candles, fairy lights or festoon lights hanging from the ceiling can have a similar effect.

FINISHING TOUCHES

Rugs

A rug can transform a space in an instant, adding colour and warmth and helping to anchor your furniture in one spot. In an open-plan space, a rug can be used to create a zone – perhaps to separate the living room from the dining area.

Before you go rug shopping, lay down sheets of newspaper to determine your ideal rug size. If you're tossing up between two sizes, go large! Ideally you want the rug to sit just under the front sofa feet, so you aren't stepping onto cold tiles or floorboards in the winter, plus a larger rug makes the rest of the room look more in proportion.

Rugs come in a lot of different materials; consider what you need for both style and practicality.

+ **Wool:** Hard-wearing and generally soft to touch, wool rugs are an excellent investment for your home. Wool rugs can shed for a number of weeks, or often months, after buying them, so you may need to vacuum the rug every few days to begin with.
+ **Acrylic/polypropylene:** These rugs are extremely hard-wearing, super soft to touch and low shedding. Because their colours and patterns are often digitally printed, they are available in a broad range of colours.
+ **Seagrass/hemp/jute/sisal:** Rugs made from natural fibres give off a relaxed coastal vibe, so are perfect choices for seaside homes. However, they tend to wear away faster than rugs in other natural materials.

Tip

Lay a rubber underlay under thin rugs that are sitting on floorboards or tiles, to stop you and the rug from slipping and sliding across the room.

Cushions

So you've splashed some serious cash on your sofa, but now you're stuck trying to work out how many scatter cushions you need and where the heck to place them? There are four key configurations to stick to when choosing and arranging cushions.

+ two square cushions at either end of the sofa
+ two square cushions at either end of the sofa, plus one rectangular cushion in the centre
+ two large square cushions and two smaller square cushions (place a large cushion at either end of the sofa, then place the smaller two in front of them)
+ five cushions spread across the sofa (mix the sizes if you like or keep them the same for symmetry)

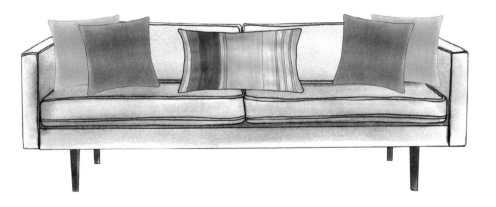

House plants

Indoor plants are great styling tools for your home as they fill in any gaps and can often work as a focal point of the room. A potted plant not only gives life to a room but also helps filter the air in the home.

Great spots for plants are beside your TV unit, on a bookshelf, by the front door or on the windowsill in your kitchen. Some even love the humidity of a steamy bathroom. Potted plants will work anywhere really, so get creative with your pots and play around with different types of plants to add some fun to your space.

Things to consider before buying a pot plant

+ Check the label on the plant to see if it likes living indoors. Some plants thrive on indoor air while others will wither and wilt in seconds, so choose wisely.
+ Different plants require different levels of light in the room. Some thrive in relatively dark spots while others ask for lots of light and sun. Consider where you intend to place your pot of greenery and then check the label.
+ Similarly, your plant will have certain requirements when it comes to temperature and humidity, and some won't thrive in air-conditioned rooms.

Tip

Some plants are harmful to young children and pets, so do your research before bringing a plant home.

Great houseplant choices

- + mother-in-law's tongue
  (also known as a snake plant)
- + fiddle leaf fig
- + dwarf olive tree
- + maidenhair ferns
- + peace lily
- + rubber plant
- + devil's ivy
- + zebra plant
- + prayer plant
- + moth orchids
- + monstera
- + zanzibar gems
- + lady palms
- + succulents
- + terrariums

Living
with pets

Our fluffy friends often dictate a lot of our decorating choices, but we shouldn't let them rule every single decision. When choosing a pet bed, opt for a neutral-coloured fabric so you can happily leave it on display in your living room or bedroom. When it comes to 'wining and dining' your pets, buy a lovely ceramic dish or bowl that co-ordinates with your colour scheme, instead of the usual bold and brash Fido-themed pet bowls on offer at the pet store. Handmade pottery items are an excellent choice for this purpose, as they tend to be more solid and robust.

For cat owners, kitty litter is a must, but it's important to keep it out of sight and especially out of range of guests' noses. Handling this aspect of cat ownership correctly can be the difference between having a cat and being a 'cat lady'. Bathrooms and laundries are often used for kitty litter storage, but a stylish litter tray will mean it's not so much of an eyesore. And if your cat likes to scratch every piece of fabric furniture in sight, then leather or synthetic leather might be a great alternative for you. The cats can't get their claws deep into the fabric weave so it's less enjoyable to scratch.

A few more handy pet tips

+ If your pet sheds its fur, choose a fabric for your sofa that has a similar tone to your pet's coat. You'll also need to invest in a good vacuum cleaner to keep the house from becoming a giant fur ball.
+ To counteract pet smells, use room sprays or reed diffusers so you and your visitors aren't greeted with doggy odour when you walk in the door.
+ To keep all your pet paraphernalia out of sight when not in use, think about allocating a specific drawer or cabinet in the entryway, kitchen or laundry for storage.

Painting
the town

There's nothing better than a fresh coat of paint to instantly lift a room, but we can't just buy one pot of paint and use it on every surface of the house. Different rooms need different types of paint.

+ Flat paint is the best choice for ceilings as it isn't reflective.
+ Matte can be tricky to work with, but is gaining popularity on internal walls.
+ Low-sheen and satin paint are good for walls. Satin has a higher gloss content, making it more durable and perfect for high-traffic areas such as hallways or living rooms.
+ Eggshell is a low-sheen paint with a similar appearance to an eggshell, as its name suggests, and is usually used on internal walls.
+ Semi-gloss paints are more durable so are a great choice for internal doors, windows and skirtings. Use them in wet areas such as bathrooms and laundries, as they can be wiped over.
+ Gloss is usually reserved for the front door.

'There's nothing
better than a
fresh coat of
paint to instantly
lift a room.'

Painting tips

You'd be very wise to engage the services of a professional when it comes to actually painting your walls, especially if painting the entire house and ceilings, but if you're up for the challenge here's a few things to keep in mind.

+ Use fresh tools – rollers, brushes and paint trays – to avoid any lumpy bits of old dried paint going onto the wall from used brushes. Cheap brushes shed hairs, which makes for a very frustrating painting experience, so don't scrimp on these.
+ Take down any curtains, mirrors and artwork before painting.
+ Fill in any holes in the walls and allow the plaster to dry prior to painting. Use fine sandpaper to sand back the plaster to ensure an even finish. If you don't do this, it will be even more obvious once you've painted it.
+ Wipe down the walls with warm water and sugar soap to remove any dust.
+ Tape up your windows, doors, trims and ceilings with blue (painter's) masking tape prior to painting. Only remove the tape once the paint is dry.
+ Always use drop sheets on the floors.
+ Start by cutting in around the edges of your walls with a brush, before using the roller to paint the entire wall.
+ Try to avoid painting in high heat or extreme cold, as the temperature will affect drying times.
+ Modern paints are mostly low in fumes but it's advisable to always have good ventilation when painting.

Dine

2/3

Dine

We have a less formal approach to dining nowadays: meals are eaten around the kitchen bench, on the coffee table or, more often than not, off our laps in front of the TV. For some, sitting at the dining table each night is still regarded as an essential part of life; for others the dining table functions as a place to eat meals, work and sort out the bills, and is only cleared off when friends come over. For those living in apartments or small houses, the dining and living areas may be combined, or perhaps there isn't room for a table at all. If you do have a dining area in your home, whether it's a separate room or part of your living area, the key element here is to create a welcoming space where you and your partner, housemates or guests will want to linger.

SPLURGE VERSUS SAVE

When it comes to buying furniture for your dining space, what do you spend your big bucks on and where do you save your pennies?

Stage 1
Big-ticket items

Start by investing in a solid timber dining table; this will carry you through numerous house moves and stages of life. A cheap dining table will only withstand one or two moves before cracking or warping, so buy once and buy well. If you have the budget, invest in a set of good-quality dining chairs as well. You can always reupholster the chairs down the track to bring the setting back on trend, or use slipcovers to hide stains.

Tip

If you can't afford to splurge on a new dining table, throw a tablecloth over your old one to hide any scratches and dents, and adorn it with a vase filled with fresh flowers.

Stage 2
Secondary items

Save your pennies on the sideboard. Instead look for one on eBay and spruce it up with a fresh coat of paint. You might even get lucky with a roadside find (keep your eyes peeled on council throw-out day).

Stage 3
Finishing touches

You don't need to splash a lot of cash on finishing touches for the room. Most homewares stores stock a range of suitable table lamps in all shapes and sizes. An attractive plant in the centre of the table or on a stand in the corner is also a nice option to consider.

A WORD ON SIZE AND PROPORTIONS

We can't cram too much furniture into the dining room, but it's important to get those few items in the room looking right. A large dining table can be an eyesore in a small room and can restrict traffic flow around the table, and a small table will look lost in a large room. Choose a table that is in proportion to the rest of the room, and make sure that there's enough room for people to get up from their chairs and walk around the table. A round or oval table could be an option if space is tight.

Tip

As there aren't a lot of items needed for a dining space, you can get away with one really striking focal point. A gorgeous pendant light or an eye-catching piece of art become great talking points while entertaining.

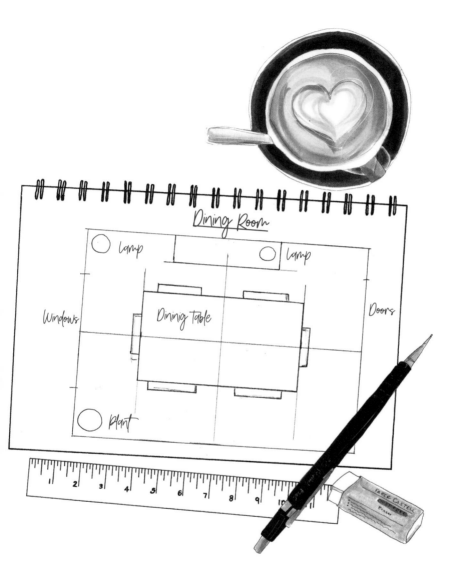

Working in
the dining room

The blending of home and work is one we often can't avoid, but how do you stylishly intertwine the two without a pile of papers inconveniently taking over your dining table?

Setting up your desk is the first step. Will it be the dining or coffee table, or do you have space for a designated desk area? If it's the former, do you have some sort of storage system, such as a buffet or sideboard, where you can put your papers away when you need to use the space for something else? If not, perhaps allocate some of your kitchen cabinet space for paper storage. You could also consider integrating your bill storage into the bookshelf in the living or dining area.

A tidy and well-ordered home office is something that is relatively within your control (especially when following a tidy routine, as suggested on pages 148–9). If your desk or home office is a mess, do you get stressed? Our physical clutter and disorganisation can cause mental clutter, especially in a work-related area, so vow to stick to a routine to ensure the mail, bills and general office paraphernalia don't get on top of you (literally and figuratively)!

LIGHTING

It's important that you provide the right lighting for your dining room. No one wants to be dropping mashed potato and gravy into their lap because they can't see what they're eating, and they don't want to be reaching for sunglasses under a set of glaring spotlights either.

+ A pendant light above the table helps to anchor and lend a sense of place to your dining area, especially in an open-plan space. However, it does mean you are limited down the track if you want to move your table to another area of the room, as the pendant will always dictate that something large should be placed underneath it.
+ A floor lamp in the corner of the dining room, beside the sideboard or buffet, will add ambience. Dim the downlights and turn the lamp on to set the mood at a dinner party.
+ Table lamps on the sideboard provide additional lighting for the dining space. They also serve as a decorative feature, adding height to the room.
+ Under-shelf lighting and pendant lights are both good task lighting options for the kitchen.

STORAGE

You can never have enough storage, and your dining room can offer lots of additional storage options. Think about putting a buffet or sideboard against the wall to store overflow china, dinnerware, glassware and board games. If you work from home, these pieces offer storage for bills, work documents and laptops. Freestanding cabinets like armoires or hutches are also a great option for additional storage. Having doors on the cabinets means you don't need to keep the shelves tidy at all times. Freestanding storage is a good option if you're renting, as the items easily move with you to the next house.

FINISHING TOUCHES

Rugs

Rugs under the dining table provide a soft texture underfoot and can add a pop of colour to the room. If you have a timber table, the rug helps to break up the amount of timber in the room, particularly if you choose a coloured or patterned rug. Rugs also provide protection against chairs scratching the floorboards when being pushed in and out.

When selecting a rug for the dining room, make sure the rug suits the size of your dining table; you don't want a huge rug that makes your table look like it's floating in the middle of its own 'rug island'. As a guideline, choose a rug that is 120–150 cm (47–59 in) wider than your table. That way you won't push your chair back and fly off the rug when standing up and sitting down.

Dining in
the living room

If your first home is the size of a shoebox and there's
not enough room for a sofa *and* a dining table, there's
no need to despair. While you can try to balance your
dinner on your lap, hopefully without staining the sofa,
there are other options for incorporating an eating area
within your living room.

+ Invest in a coffee table with storage underneath.
  That way you can clear the top of the coffee table
  to make way for your Uber Eats delivery, and use
  the coffee table as your servery.
+ Plate up your takeaway into bowls and serve them
  on the coffee table, complete with placemats
  and napkins. Pull the cushions off the sofa and
  use them as floor cushions. Pretend you're having
  an indoor picnic.
+ Buy a few extra trays to place on your side table.
  Then you can pop your cutlery, napkin and water
  glass on the tray with your dinner plate or bowl, and
  move the tray from the table to your lap without
  spilling. For those playing at home, this is *not* the
  TV dinner tray you see in US sitcoms from the '90s.
  This is the grown-up version.

Don't forget your kitchen island bench can do double duty as a zone for eating meals. Most kitchen benches will need 65 cm (25½ in) high stools; don't go much higher than that or your knees will bang into the top of the bench.

All in all, the key here is to make your dining situation, whatever it may be, a comfy and cosy one. It's important for our health and happiness that we take time out from our busy lives to sit down and connect with our family and friends. If that means sitting on the floor to eat your dinner, so be it.

A WORD ON KITCHENS

Okay, let's be real here. If cooking really isn't your thing or if you know your pizza delivery driver better than your neighbours, you probably aren't going to need the latest and greatest of every kitchen appliance and utensil ever invented. But you do want your kitchen to have the basics for when friends pop over for brunch or for when you do feel like cooking up a storm.

Things one must have in the kitchen to look sophisticated

+ dinner set and cutlery for four people
+ wine glasses, champagne glasses (if you're feeling classy) and water glasses (keep hydrated, kids!)
+ mugs
+ tea strainer
+ chopping board
+ knife block
+ cheese knives – for your cheeseboards, of course
+ salad bowl and servers
+ platters
+ mixing bowls
+ bakeware: muffin tin, cake tin, baking/roasting tin
+ tupperware and other storage containers
+ saucepan set and frying pan
+ casserole dish
+ kettle and toaster
+ electric beaters
+ spiraliser – for those of you who are super fancy and only eat zucchini (courgette) noodles instead of pasta
+ corkscrew
+ can opener
+ kitchen tongs
+ ladle
+ potato masher
+ vegetable peeler
+ fruit bowl
+ lemon juicer
+ placemats
+ tea towels (dish towels)
+ oven mits
+ bin

Decor tips that won't break the bank

+ Rehome certain packet foods – pasta, flour, sugar and tea – into attractive storage jars. That way you can leave them on the kitchen bench or shelf for decoration.
+ If your kitchen is a little bland, think of jazzing it up with funky tea towels or colourful artwork.
+ Statement kettles and toasters are fun accessories you can leave out on the bench.
+ If you have limited drawer space, try housing your kitchen utensils in an attractive pot.
+ You can't go wrong with a vase of fresh flowers or a bowl of fruit on the kitchen bench.

Sanctuary – Dine

Balcony
herb garden

A small herb garden is a lovely addition to your outdoor balcony or courtyard and provides a year-round herb supply when cooking. You'll feel like a boss as you head out to your balcony to pluck a few sprigs of fresh parsley for your pasta or some mint for your mojitos, instead of having to remember them on your shopping list each week. This is also a quick way of making a rental property more homely.

Hanging
art

Artwork on the walls can provide the focal point for your room and really bring everything together.

A few general guidelines

+ Artwork should be at eye level. Most people tend to hang artwork about 20 cm (8 in) too high, which ends up throwing off the rest of the room proportionally. The average eye level is about 150 cm (60 in) from the ground up, so that is the best spot to centre your art on the wall. If you have high ceilings, add 10–20 cm (4–8 in).
+ If you're hanging art above a sofa, add 60–70 cm (24–28 in) from the top of the sofa to the bottom of the artwork, to avoid hitting your head against the edge of the frame when you lean back. You want your artwork to be at least half the length of your sofa but often three-quarters is better proportionally. Anything narrower in width will look too small for the room.
+ If you're hanging art above a piece of furniture you don't need to sit on, allow about 20 cm (8 in) of space.
+ If your wall has items like light switches or air-conditioning controls, you'll want to centre the artwork in line with these.
+ If you're in doubt about size when choosing artwork, go larger rather than smaller. The room won't look disjointed when using large art pieces but small artworks can make the scale of the room look a little off.
+ Lots of different artworks or frames scattered randomly across a wall can look a bit of a mess. One solution is to hang a gallery wall, which can bring all these different elements together. It's the perfect way to display lots of family photos or perhaps photos from your travels overseas. To avoid any annoying mistakes when arranging the items on the wall, use paper or newspaper cut-outs in the same sizes as your art pieces and arrange them on the floor in front of the wall until you're happy with the composition.

Tools you'll need

+ hooks
+ hammer
+ spirit level

+ tape measure
+ pencil

Tips for renters

We all want to personalise our space with a few colourful artworks, and just because you're renting doesn't mean you should miss out. Here are a few tips for hanging art – and you'll still get your bond back.

+ Picture-hanging strips and hooks with sticky backs are a renter's best friend. They come in lots of different sizes and can accommodate different weights. Just peel them off on moving day.
+ Stretch a piece of wire or string from one point to another and use it to display postcards, paper artwork or photos. Use mini pegs or paper clips to attach the items to the wire.
+ Lean your artwork up against the wall. This gives a casual vibe to the room and you can easily change the artwork around when you want to refresh the decor.
+ Hang posters or lightweight artworks on your walls using Blu Tack or Japanese washi tape. These both peel off easily without leaving holes in the walls or tearing the paint.

'We all want to personalise our space with a few colourful artworks, and just because you're renting doesn't mean you should miss out.'

Sleep

Sleep

Possibly the room with the highest score on the cosiness scale, our bedrooms are our havens, a place where we allow ourselves to rest and recharge. It's where we retreat to when things get a little tough, where we recuperate when we're unwell and where we engage in some less restful activities, too ... Just because you aren't inviting all your guests into your bedroom (or maybe you are, no judgement), doesn't mean you don't have to worry about how you decorate it. It's a multifunctional space where you sleep, get ready for the day, read a book in the evenings, or relax with a cup of coffee and a significant other on weekend mornings, so it needs a fair bit of attention to meet all those needs. Following are some ideas to help turn your bedroom into the sophisticated sanctuary that you deserve.

SPLURGE VERSUS SAVE

Not sure where to start when it comes to buying furniture for the bedroom? Use this guide to help steer you in the right direction.

Stage 1
Big-ticket items

This is pretty obvious but let's spell it out anyway. Your bed needs to be one of the first things you buy. When buying a bed, it's a good idea to invest in a mattress at the same time: buy the best mattress your budget will allow – it will have a huge impact on the quality of your sleep. Once the bed and mattress are sorted, then choose your bedside tables. If storage is an issue, go for tables with shelves or cupboards.

Tip

When hunting around for design ideas for your bedroom, use hotel rooms as your inspiration. Have you ever stayed in a hotel room you never wanted to leave? What was it about the room that made you want to stay?

Stage 2
Secondary items

Once the bed is in place, choose your rugs, armchairs and bed ottomans. Opt for mid-range here – you don't need to spend a fortune on these things.

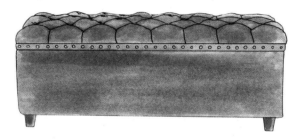

Stage 3
Finishing touches

Save on the smaller items such as bedside lamps, scatter cushions or artwork. These are things you can replace a few years down the track (without breaking the bank) when you're ready for a style change. Some finishing touches are best to splurge on: to really make your bedroom feel hotel-worthy, invest in good-quality linen and a doona.

LIGHTING

Getting the lighting right in your bedroom is rather important: too bright and you'll hate spending any time in there at night, too dark and you'll send yourself blind trying to read in bed in the evenings. The trick is to use several layers of light: bright lights for when you want to get dressed, task lighting for reading or putting on make-up, and mood lighting for relaxing in bed.

+ You want your ceiling light to be bright enough for daily tasks, especially in the evenings or dark winter mornings when there's no natural light. Where possible, have a dimmer switch installed so you can control the light levels and create some mood lighting when needed.
+ If having a dimmer switch isn't an option, make sure your table lamps have a higher wattage light bulb installed, so you can turn the overhead lights off, but still get enough light into the room for reading or getting dressed.
+ Anglepoise lamps are perfect for reading in bed, because they allow you to direct the light where it's needed.
+ Choose your bedside lamp bulb carefully. Is the bulb on display? If so, pick a pretty bulb not an ugly standard supermarket bulb.
+ If the inner workings of your lamp are on display and not particularly attractive, ensure your shade covers the bulb; you want the shade to be the feature, not the insides of the lamp.

Sanctuary — Sleep

Window
treatments

For light-sensitive sleepers, getting your bedroom window treatments sorted is a top priority. A room that is too light at night can result in poor-quality sleep. Good-quality curtains help to insulate the room, keeping it warmer in winter and cooler in summer. Curtains also have the ability to soften a window and dress up a bedroom.

If privacy is an issue, think about installing a double-track curtain rail. A sheer curtain at the back will control natural light in the day and provide some privacy, while allowing you to draw blackout curtains in the front while sleeping.

Roller or roman blinds are an alternative to curtains. Roller blinds are often not as decorative or attractive as curtains and may not provide full blackout because light can still seep through either side of the rollers. Plantation shutters are also popular in bedrooms but, again, these don't guarantee full light exclusion. Hanging a curtain over the top of them can counteract this.

Tip

Hang your curtains at the ceiling, not directly above the window, to create the illusion of high ceilings.

STORAGE

The bedroom can become a dumping ground at times, and if you haven't got much storage in the room you'll need to get creative in order to avoid total chaos.

+ **Walk-in or built-in wardrobe:** If you are lucky enough to have one of these, most of your storage problems will be solved. They usually have a clever mix of hanging and drawer space, as well as a designated area for shoes. Extra shelving or cupboards are great for storing seasonal items such as winter coats and beach towels.
+ **Shoe-storage system:** Wall-mounted shoe racks or cupboards are cost-effective space-saving solutions. If you don't have room in the bedroom, then these can be placed at the entryway instead. Alternatively, hang a pocket shoe hanger in your wardrobe or on the back of the door – these can house up to ten pairs of shoes.
+ **Chest of drawers:** Not only are these great for smaller items such as t-shirts, socks, undergarments and any other items that can be folded, but placing a chest of drawers opposite the end of your bed brings a sense of symmetry to the room.
+ **Bedside tables:** Opt for tables with drawers for overflow storage.
+ **Multipurpose furniture:** A storage ottoman at the end of the bed is great for extra bed linen and is a good spot to perch while you slip your shoes on or off.
+ **Under-bed storage:** A bed with a gas-lift mechanism or built-in drawers allows plenty of additional storage.
+ **Hooks:** Over-the-door hook racks are great for hanging things like dressing gowns, a winter coat and handbags.

Tip

Bedroom chairs often end up becoming a visual display of the outfits you've worn all week. Avoid the dumping ground by placing a laundry hamper or basket next to the chair.

BEDROOM FOCAL POINTS

Bedheads

This is the most obvious focal point for your bedroom, and your options here are almost endless. You could choose a grand bed with a built-in bedhead, or perhaps even a four-poster or canopy bed. Otherwise, if you have an ensemble base, consider some of these alternative bedhead ideas:

+ padded or buttoned fabric
+ ornate gates hung on the wall (these function as both bedhead and art)
+ old windows or reclaimed wooden doors
+ a pair of wooden window shutters
+ an Indian or Chinese carved wooden screen
+ washi tape outline on the wall
+ painted pieces of MDF

Typically you want your bedhead to be at least 150 cm (59 in) high, but ceiling height will affect your choices. If you have tall ceilings you can go higher with the bedhead, but if your ceilings are relatively low, a giant bedhead will crowd the room and make it feel smaller.

Tip

Be kind to your housemates (or neighbours!) before you engage in a little horizontal dancing by making sure that your bed base is screwed in properly, or that your ensemble base is sturdy enough to prevent the bedhead banging against the wall.

Art

The right artwork can add the perfect finishing touch to the bedroom. Hang your artwork directly above and centred to the bed (landscape or square art, or even a triptych, works best here), or hang two portrait pieces on either side of the bedhead, above the bedside tables. Alternatively, hang the artwork on the wall opposite the bed so you can see it when you're lying down.

Mirror

Opt for a full-length mirror so you can check yourself out each morning when getting ready for the day. Or hang a mirror above your chest of drawers to bounce some extra morning light into the room from the window opposite.

Wallpaper

Go for a more luxurious touch by wallpapering the entire wall behind your bedhead. If you like getting creative with your bed linen, then it's best to opt for a more subdued and subtle wallpaper pattern so you can play around with bolder colours on the bed.

'Hang a mirror
to bounce some
extra morning light
into the room from
the window opposite.'

Disguising the TV

People have very strong opinions on this one; it's either a resounding yes or a no when it comes to having a TV in the bedroom. Some studies have shown that watching TV before bed or while in bed reduces your sleep quality, but if you (or your partner) insists then at least try to minimise the impact it has on the look of the room. A big black box staring at you from the wall isn't exactly the nicest focal point for a bedroom.

+ Place the TV on top of a beautiful chest of drawers. To draw your eye away from the TV, consider a bone inlay chest of drawers or one with some decorative features painted on it – something that will really catch your attention.
+ Mount it on the wall opposite your bed to minimise the distraction from your decor.
+ Paint the wall a dark colour to help the TV blend into the background a bit more.
+ Hide it behind sliding wardrobe doors or inside a cupboard such as an armoire.

Bedside
basics

The height of your bedside table is important for practicality. You don't want to be reaching up high to grab a drink of water in the night, nor do you want to be stretching almost to the ground either. As you will be placing a bedside lamp on top of the table, you'll want to ensure the light is shining at the right level for reading in bed. If your bedside table is taller than average (50–60 cm/20–24 in), then you will need a shorter lamp to compensate.

Bear in mind the height of your mattress as well. Ideally your bedside table should be in line with the top of your mattress, but pillow-top mattresses, which are popular these days, are quite a bit higher than ordinary mattresses. It's a good idea to measure the height of your ensemble base and mattress before buying your bedside tables to avoid disappointment.

FINISHING TOUCHES

Bed linen

There's lots to keep in mind when choosing bed linen. Natural materials such as cotton are so much nicer to sleep on – anything with a polyester blend may make you sweat/perspire/glow in your sleep. When it comes to colour, choose crisp white fitted and flat sheets for that hotel-room vibe. Or get funky by pairing mismatched colours, such as a dusty pink fitted sheet with a light grey top sheet. Go for a patterned doona cover if your room is already full of neutrals and needs some jazzing up, or opt for a neutral linen and play around with fun scatter cushions instead.

Cotton

Cotton is the most common material for sheets. It is a soft, natural material that is breathable and cosy for sleeping on. Typically you can expect to see three types of cotton sheets:

+ Organic cotton is grown without toxic pesticide use or synthetic fertilisers.
+ Pima cotton is a soft and durable cotton developed in the USA. This type of cotton has similar qualities to Egyptian cotton but is not as expensive.
+ Egyptian cotton is the highest-quality cotton and therefore the most expensive. This cotton is traditionally grown in Egypt, but is now often grown in China or India from cotton plants originating from Egypt. Mostly the manufacturer won't list the origin of their cotton plants, so it's hard to tell what you'll be getting (although if the price is too good to be true then you probably aren't buying authentic Egyptian cotton).

Linen

Linen is a material woven from the flax plant and is typically more expensive than most other bedding materials due to the laborious nature of weaving the flax fibres. Linen is a nice choice in the warmer months as it keeps you cooler than other materials. Because linen has a more open weave, be aware that fitted bottom sheets can start to stretch over time.

Flannelette

Flannelette is a cotton fabric that has been brushed on one side to create a soft feel. Flannelette sheets are a heavier weight than cotton sheets, making them a perfect choice for winter.

Silk

Silk is made by silkworms to create a super-luxurious thread. Mulberry silk is the highest-quality silk, as it's made from worms that are fed only mulberry leaves. The front side of a silk sheet is glossy while the back is duller. (Satin is a man-made version of silk and not as high quality.) The advantages of silk sheets are that they are hypoallergenic and very cool for summer. Silk pillowcases are claimed to prevent facial wrinkles and keep hair frizz-free while sleeping. You be the judge.

Thread counts

High thread counts don't always necessarily translate to luxuriousness or superior quality. The thread count is purely the number of threads woven per square inch of fabric. In order to claim the sheets as 1000 thread count, some manufacturers twist lower-quality threads into multiple threads to give them more strength. This increases the number of threads per square inch but doesn't necessarily improve the quality of the sheet. As a general rule, buying a set of sheets with a thread count of 400 will still offer you a very comfortable night's sleep.

Tip

Mattress toppers are the secret to getting a hotel-worthy bed at home. The mattress topper is easily removed to be washed or fluffed up each time you make the bed.

Summer versus winter bedding

In summer, opt for natural materials against your skin. Linen is particularly nice but cotton is also an excellent choice. All you generally need in summer is a fitted sheet, top sheet and cotton waffle blanket. A lightweight doona for the beginning and end of the season will keep you warm as the nights start to turn cooler.

In winter, a wool or feather and down doona will keep you warm and cosy. For added warmth, have a wool blanket close by. Choose flannelette sheets if you live in a particularly cold climate.

An ottoman at the end of your bed with some hidden storage will give you somewhere to store your bed linen in the off season.

Pillows

You don't want to look like a crazy pillow person, but nor do you want your bed to look like a barren wasteland. As a basic guide, when styling a double or queen bed, you'll want to work with:

+ either four standard pillows,
+ or two standard and two European pillows (these large, square pillows are placed at the back of the bed for a luxe look),
+ plus one or two (or three …) scatter cushions.

When arranging the pillows on your bed, go from big to small.

+ Start with two European pillows (60 x 60 cm/24 x 24 in). You can lean against these when reading or enjoying breakfast in bed.
+ Then add two or four standard pillows (if you aren't using Euro pillows, then go with four pillows here). These are the pillows you actually sleep on.
+ Finish off the bed with two square scatter cushions (45 x 45 cm/ 18 x 18 in). These may be considered annoying to the majority of the male population, but adding scatter cushions to the bed can bring life to your room. However, it's best not to overdo it; stick to one or two cushions to inject some colour and fun into your bedroom scheme.
+ If you like, add a decorative lumbar cushion (35 x 60 cm/ 14 x 24 in).

Tip

To finish off your bed's outfit, consider a valance. This wraps around the base of an ensemble mattress to dress it up.

How to make your bed in under 30 seconds

+ Pull the top sheet up to the pillows and fold it down to sit under the pillows.
+ Pull the doona up to the pillows. Place the pillows on top of the doona.
+ Place your scatter cushions on top of the doona, in front of the pillows, and away you go.

Rugs

The placement of your bedroom rug should be practical as well as aesthetically pleasing. Ideally, the rug should take up three-quarters of the bed space – it should extend 30–40 cm (12–16 in) beyond the end and sides of the bed, so that when you hop out of bed in the morning your feet touch the rug not the floor. Ideal bedroom rug materials are wool, wool and silk, polypropylene and sheepskins, as they are softer underfoot than materials such as hemp, sisal, seagrass and jute.

If you don't want to buy a full-size rug for the room, consider two small rugs on either side of the bed – a soft fluffy sheepskin rug is particularly luxurious.

SHARING A BEDROOM

The ultimate compromise in life: decorating your bedroom with a significant other. Whose style and taste wins out? How do you decide? Fight it out and let the best man win … or find a compromise?

First consider if there are adequate storage facilities for you both to comfortably live in this room. If not, is there another bedroom with a wardrobe you can 'borrow'? Or can you add strategic storage like a shoe cabinet at the front entryway, or swap out a small chest of drawers in the bedroom for a larger one for you both to use? Think about bedside tables, bed ottomans, wooden chests or pull-out containers under the bed as places for extra clothes storage.

Reading lights are a must if one of you likes sitting up in bed with a good book until all hours while the other is sound asleep by 9 pm. Anglepoise lamps are good for reading and won't disturb your sleeping partner, while tall standard lamps are better for overall lighting.

If you or your partner tends to be the one to take over the decorating, how do you ensure the other is still happy with the outcome? While you may not always like their decorating choices, it's important that both parties are represented in the room, whether it be treasured family photos, sporting memorabilia or souvenirs collected on various travels.

Does one person have an obsession with dusty pink but the other person prefers a more neutral scheme? Perhaps instead of that pink floral quilt cover, go for a neutral colour and add a pop of pink with your scatter cushions. If you stick to a relatively neutral colour palette overall, you can then inject colour and individuality into the room with soft furnishings such as rugs, curtains and bed linen. It's all about blending!

SHARING A BATHROOM

Sharing a bedroom with a significant other for the first time may take some adjustments, but sharing a bathroom comes with a whole new set of rules and regulations. Heck, sharing a bathroom with housemates is fraught with anxiety too!

Work out who gets which drawers or cupboards, and buy some little storage tubs or baskets to collate each person's bathroom toiletries and odds and ends. That way Joe's toothpaste isn't going to end up all over Sally's hairbrush and Jane's bobby pins will never go missing (well, that's a lie, those things have a mind of their own).

A weekly cleaning schedule helps keep everyone sane in a shared bathroom situation. Write up the recurring to-dos and tape it to the fridge. Everyone takes turns completing the to-do list and hopefully in the process no one gets hurt. If you live with a lazy partner or housemates who don't care for cleaning, you may have to cough up for a cleaner to visit weekly or fortnightly so it doesn't fall to one person to do. The same goes for items that everyone uses, such as toilet paper and tissues; add these to a 'house shopping list' that is then divided between the housemates.

Lovely
laundries

The laundry is not the most exciting room in the house, that's for sure, but it's definitely a practical one. There's no reason why you can't add a little bit of lovely to your laundry. Here are a few styling tips:

+ Decant your washing powder into a pretty tin that can happily sit on the laundry bench.
+ Buy a rattan or woven basket for your laundry. Ensure it has a lid so you don't have to look at dirty clothes every time you walk into the room.
+ Hang some art on the walls, because ... why not? If you have a spare wall that isn't taken up with a washing machine or cupboards, then hang a framed picture to make the room a little more inviting.
+ Apothecary-style bottles are a nice touch next to the sink for your hand soap, fabric softener and other laundry liquids.
+ If you have lots of open shelves in your laundry, you could dedicate some space for towels or linen storage. Fold and display your towels in colour groupings.

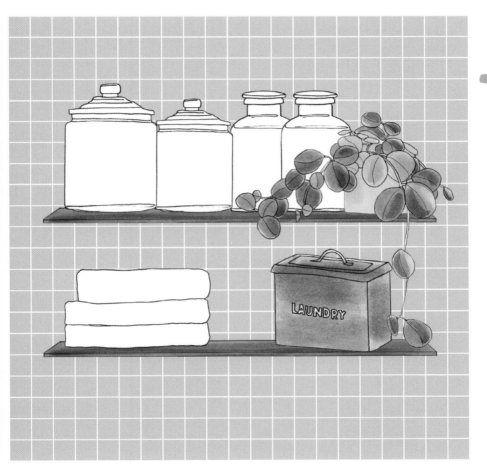

Crystals
in the home

Crystals have been used for thousands of years for their healing energies and magic powers. They are thought to have the power to cleanse the polluted energy from the electrical devices in your home, such as the TV, microwave, wi-fi and computers, helping to bring peace to your room. They also make wonderful decorative items. There is a different crystal for every time and place – and also every colour scheme! Try grouping them on your coffee table, on a small tray on your bedside table, or in a giant bowl on your dining table.

Before you start working with your crystal, it's important that you cleanse it of any negative energy that it may have picked up on its journey to you. There are a few ways to do this, such as placing it in the sunlight or moonlight (especially powerful during a full moon) or holding it under running water for at least one minute.

Crystals in the bedroom

To help create a good energy in your bedroom, think about putting a small bowl of crystals on the bedside table or chest of drawers.

+ **Rose quartz:** Also known as the love stone, this aids the flow of love.
+ **Malachite:** Thought to reduce stress and assist with better-quality sleep and dream interpretation.
+ **Jade:** Increases longevity and fertility, and brings balance, compassion and peace.
+ **Howlite:** A calming stone, good for easing insomnia.
+ **Rhodochrosite:** A powerful healing stone, assisting with memory enhancement, divine love and healing love wounds.

Crystals in the living room

Lots of heated family debate can happen in the living room, so this room will benefit from some crystal love.

+ **Clear quartz:** The mother of all crystals, this will aid with positive family discussions.
+ **Turquoise:** Will help to diffuse the negative energy from the electrical devices in your living room.
+ **Sodalite:** This stone enhances communications and alleviates fears; it brings a sense of clarity and calmness.
+ **Fluorite:** A clearing stone, assisting with decluttering the mind of confusion and negativity. It is helpful for when you need to act impartially.
+ **Ruby fuchsite:** Aids in clearing blockages of the heart; it encourages you to face the future with trust, confidence and positivity.

Crystals in the home office

This space can store a lot of stress and negative energy, especially if you have a high-power job and work late into the night.

+ **Amethyst:** This stone will help to keep the space calm and cleansed of bad vibes.
+ **Citrine:** To attract abundance and promote alignment, enhancing creative imagination and clarity of thought.
+ **Aventurine:** Great for creativity, relaxation, motivation and leadership.
+ **Peridot:** The stone of financial abundance, it aids in attracting our vision. This is a very helpful stone for business.
+ **Tiger's eye:** The 'go for it' stone; helps dispel worry and activates intelligence. It energises the mind to achieve harmony and balance.

Tip

Crystals aren't the only things to shift the energy in your home. Salt lamps and sage smudge sticks can also help clear up any negative energy.

Celebration

I love any excuse
to throw a party.

If a friend's birthday is coming up, I'll start making lists about a month beforehand: what type of food to serve, ideas for a theme and decorations, the invitation list ... For Christmas it's my job to style and decorate the table. I spend weeks planning the decor: the colour scheme, flowers, place cards, how to coordinate the Christmas crackers with the table setting – the whole shebang. I think I love the planning process just as much as the party itself!

As children, birthdays were always cause for a big celebration in my family (and they still are!). A few weeks out from the day, Mum would hand my brothers or me the much-loved birthday cake recipe book and we would pore over the pages, trying to decide which cake we wanted. The excitement on the day of the party was always intense. Mum would be busy adding all the important details – setting the table with coordinating tablecloths and napkins, hanging the balloons and streamers – while I paced around the house in my party dress, impatiently waiting for the first guest to arrive. Thanks to Mum, the day was always a success, and everyone left with smiles on their faces and a goodie bag full of sugary treats, to extend the party high just that little bit longer.

Nowadays I focus less on birthday cakes and sugar highs, but the reason for celebrating remains the same: to connect with my family and friends away from the everyday stresses of life and work, to indulge in a fabulous feast and, of course, to set up a beautiful table brimming with flowers and decorations.

However, putting on a big production for your nearest and dearest does come with its challenges, and people often ask me for ideas or advice when planning their own soirées at home. Hopefully this section will answer some of your questions, give you a few ideas and, importantly, give you the confidence to plan your own special celebration with family and friends.

ENTERTAINING AND THE FIVE SENSES

Asking people over to your home to celebrate a milestone, job promotion or the birth of a new baby is all about showing that you love and appreciate them. We show we care through the food and wine we serve, the flowers on the table, the balloons and other decorations. However, there are other, less tangible, things to consider as well – all five senses should be taken into account.

Sight

It's a fairly obvious point, but a clean, tidy space is much more inviting than a home overtaken by mess and in desperate need of a dust. You don't need to spend half the day cleaning, but have a quick run around with the vacuum in the morning or the day before, and make sure rooms such as the bathroom and toilet are clean. Replace the hand towels and put out a fresh hand soap. If you have time, quickly mop over the kitchen and bathroom floors.

Touch

What will your guests be sitting on? What fabrics will you be using on the table? Are you offering paper napkins or linen ones? Take the weather into consideration as well; heat or cool the house adequately to ensure no one is shivering in a corner or sweating profusely under their party attire. All of these elements play a role in your guests' overall experience.

Sound

Sound, or music, plays such a vital role in creating ambiance and atmosphere. Start with some light tunes playing in the background until everyone gets comfortable – no one wants to be stuck staring at a stranger in absolute silence – and then amp up the volume and tempo a bit as the party gets going. It's a good idea to plan your party playlist beforehand.

Taste

This is not an element of entertaining to be overlooked. Food is important and something your guests will remember. If cooking is not your forte, think about outsourcing some of the catering.

Smell

The smell of your cooking wafting through the house is a nice teaser for guests of what's to come. Also consider lighting some candles to scent the house if you're cooking something with a strong aroma or you need to get rid of the pet smell in the apartment. Fresh scented flowers are also an excellent addition to the room.

Tip

Throw the doors and windows open (so long as it's not the middle of winter) at least an hour before you're expecting guests, to get some fresh air flowing through the rooms.

WHEN GUESTS POP OVER

Do you have a friend who calls and says they are five minutes away and that they're just going to pop over for a quick cup of tea and a catch up? Those words can strike fear and panic in even the most organised among us. Here's what you should have on hand so that everyone thinks you're a total domestic god/goddess:

+ **Tea and coffee supplies:** Stock a range of tea bags to keep everyone happy – herbal, green, Earl Grey, English breakfast. Decaf coffee or chai tea might score you extra points.
+ **Biscuits:** A good go-to is shortbread, biscotti or chocolate chip biscuits. If you're a clever cook, keep some cookie dough in the freezer. When friends say they're on their way, simply turn on the oven, slice the dough into rounds, and you'll have a batch of warm home-made cookies on the table by the time they arrive. Bonus points: the house will smell amazing!
+ **Crackers and dip:** These are perfect for an impromptu afternoon or evening snack, especially with a few carrot and celery sticks.
+ **Tinned soup:** This makes a quick and easy lunch. Empty the contents of the tin into a small saucepan to heat, and sprinkle with dried herbs to make it look home-made.
+ **Wine:** Keep a few bottles in the cabinet or the fridge, just in case.

Tip

Turn to page 149 for some simple tricks to get your house looking neat and tidy when you've only got a few moments to spare before a guest arrives.

Celebration

WHEN GUESTS STAY OVER

Celebration

Whether you've got friends visiting for one night or the mother-in-law is staying for a week, it pays to plan ahead.

+ If you know you've got guests staying overnight, particularly if they've been travelling, make up their bed in advance. Tired guests arriving in the evening will appreciate not having to make their own bed before hitting the hay.
+ If you have the luxury of a spare room, always have the bed ready to go, just in case anyone needs to stay overnight or turns up at short notice.
+ If your guests are sleeping on a pull-out sofa in the living room, offer them an eye mask and ear plugs in case the window treatments aren't adequate for light or sound control.
+ Put a towel and face towel on the bed – then your guests will feel comfortable about taking a shower whenever they're ready.
+ If your visitors are staying for a few days, clear out some space in the wardrobe for hanging clothes.
+ Pop a jug of water and some glasses by the bed, along with a note with the wi-fi password.
+ A small vase of fresh flowers and a scented candle are lovely welcoming touches to the room.

Tip

One of the greatest gifts you can offer your guests is a 'go with the flow' attitude. If you feel stressed, so will they. Making your guests feel relaxed and welcome is the key to success.

Moving on from
the house party

Some of the best things about the teenage years are house parties. But what happens when we all grow up, move into our own place and decide we'd like to ask some friends over for a few drinks? What happens to house parties then? Well, they grow up, too.

While we can now meet friends and catch up in any restaurant, bar or pub we want, there are times when we'd rather socialise in the comfort of our own homes. But asking people into your space and knowing how to 'feed, water and entertain' them can be daunting, particularly for a first-timer.

Hosting any sort of celebration will undoubtedly come with some level of stress, but the key here is to keep it casual. A weekend barbecue is probably your best option. These are low-key affairs that won't require too much preparation in advance, and if you ask everyone to bring a salad, then you won't be spending half the night in the kitchen drowning in a sea of lettuce leaves and vinaigrette. Once you've nailed the barbecue and got a few gold stars on the board, you can ramp it up next time with a 'dinner party for grown-ups' – this is where you can really flex your entertaining muscles!

PARTY PLANNING

Hosting any sort of celebration will undoubtedly come with some level of stress. To help make the occasion memorable for your guests and smooth and stress-free for yourself, a little bit of pre-party planning is essential.

We all lead busy lives, so often setting the date and sending out the invitations is about as far as our preparation goes. Don't be the host that leaves all the shopping, cleaning and outfit planning to the day of the event! The more you can do in advance the less stressed you'll be on the day. You'll also want to be able to enjoy the time with your guests, rather than spending the entire evening in the kitchen doing things you could have done the day before.

Sit down the week beforehand and plan a few key details. This also helps you identify what you could potentially outsource to other people to help make your life easier. You don't have to plan every detail, but an overall plan helps significantly.

A checklist is your best friend. Write one out for both the lead-up to the day and the day itself, and keep them handy so you can add to them whenever anything else pops into your head.

Tip

Do you have twelve people for dinner but your dinner set is only for eight? To avoid last-minute panic, do an inventory check on your cutlery, plates, wine glasses – even chairs!

'Leading up to the event' checklist

+ Set the date and time for the party.
+ Write the guest list.
+ Send out the invitations.
+ If your party has a set theme, consider any special decorations you might need to source or make.
+ Plan your outfit.
+ Plan your menu and cocktail/drinks list.
+ Figure out any dishes you can buy, prepare in advance or outsource to your guests.
+ Find a time to do the grocery shopping and plan a visit to the flower markets.
+ Call a handyman or hone your DIY skills if there's anything around the house that needs fixing before you have guests over.
+ Put together your music playlist.
+ Call, visit or send a note to any neighbours who need forewarning that you're entertaining.

'On the day' checklist

+ Visit the flower markets first thing in the morning and sprinkle some flower love throughout the house.
+ Cook or bake any dishes you can't make in advance, and prepare any food you'll be making once guests arrive.
+ Put the wine and beer in the fridge. If there's no room, buy bags of ice to keep drinks cool.
+ Empty all bins and replace the bin liners.
+ Put any pet paraphernalia (dog beds, pet toys, kitty litter) out of sight.
+ Place out any extra bins for collecting bottles and recycling.
+ Do a final tidy up, concentrating on the bathroom, kitchen and any rooms your guests will likely be spending a lot of time in.
+ Light candles and fluff up your sofa cushions.

Celebration

Invitations

Sending out invites doesn't have to be super formal; it could just be an email to your group of friends with the details of your event. Or go all out and send pretty paper invitations by snail mail. Be sure to include the date, time, location, RSVP details and any other important information such as BYO or 'bring a plate'. If your party is themed or you're hosting it in a venue that has a dress code, be sure to communicate that to your guests. No one wants to be the person who turns up underdressed.

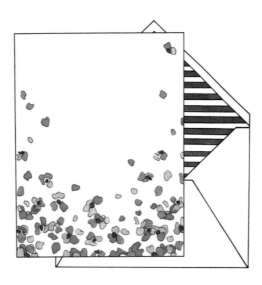

Party planning on a budget

How do you successfully cater for all your friends and have a good time without breaking the budget? Here are a few handy hints to keep you from going bankrupt.

+ **Pantry edit:** What have you already got in the fridge or pantry that you can use? Or what can you make that only requires you to buy a handful of things to cater adequately?
+ **Recycle themes:** Do you have leftover party decorations from another party you hosted? Can you recycle some of these items or re-purpose them? Also consider asking friends to bring along decor items to help you out.
+ **Check your place settings:** To save on splurging for new dinnerware you don't particularly need, why not ask a friend to bring some extra plates and glasses. If you don't have enough large platters or bowls to serve your dishes in, trawl your local op shop to pick up some inexpensive options.
+ **Bring a plate:** Catering for a large group is an expensive event. Instead, ask each guest to bring something. Bonus: it also saves you a few hours slaving away in the kitchen. (For more tips on bring-a-plate entertaining, see page 195.)

Celebration

Tip

Make sure you always have pantry staples such as spices, oils, vinegars, sauces and dressings, so that you can make some basic recipes based on the other ingredients you have in the house.

There are so many reasons to throw a party. Use the ideas below as a starting point for your party decorations, food and drink planning.

+ Alice in Wonderland tea party
+ Baby shower
+ Chinese New Year
+ Dinner party
+ Easter
+ Fourth of July
+ Game night (gather to watch a big sporting game
  – or perhaps board games are more your thing?)
+ Housewarming
+ Italian pizza party
+ Jumping castle (yes, they've got them for adults, too)
+ Kitchen tea/bridal shower
+ Lazy Sunday brunch (who doesn't love a mimosa?)
+ Mexicarnivale
+ New Year's Eve
+ Old Hollywood glamour
+ Pink party (serve all the food on pink plates along
  with the prettiest rosé or sparking rosé you can find)
+ Queen's Birthday celebration
+ Rock star party
+ Sushi dinner
+ Thanksgiving
+ Unicorn party (get your rainbows and fairy dust on!)
+ Valentine's Day
+ Wine and cheese night
+ Xbox party
+ Yoga and health food
+ Zombie party

Tip

Is your home a 'shoes off' home?
If yes, make sure you let guests
know in advance. That way they
won't be caught off guard and
have to spend the night walking
around with their big toe
sticking out of holey socks.

ETIQUETTE

The perfect host

+ If you are expecting timely guests you'll need to ensure the food is served in a timely manner as well. Consider outsourcing and ordering in if you're worried that you won't have enough time to cook everything. We're all busy; your guests won't mind if you've taken a few shortcuts.
+ 'Plus ones' are always tricky territory. If you really don't have room to accommodate a plus one you'll need to make it clear beforehand. If you're opening up your backyard to one and all, then unannounced extra guests won't be too much of an imposition.
+ If you know one of your guests is attending on their own and may not know the rest of the group, introduce them to – or seat them beside – someone you think they'll get along with. But a word of warning: never use a sit-down dinner party as an excuse to match-make two friends without letting the said parties know prior to arrival – it can be a recipe for disaster.
+ Clearing the table can indicate to your guests that you're ready for the party to end. If that's not the case, make a suggestion that they move to the lounge area for an after-dinner drink. This will save any confusion as to whether you want them to leave or not.
+ If you think your friend has had too much to drink and really shouldn't drive, offer to call an Uber or suggest they sleep the night. If you don't have a spare room, a bottom sheet and a cotton waffle blanket with a pillow on the sofa should be enough for a relatively comfortable sleep for your impromptu guest.

Celebration

Technology
at the table

These days it's the norm to see phones gracing the top of cafe and restaurant tables during meals. But if you're invited to someone's house, keep your phone in your bag or pocket. Be present and involved in the conversations around you rather than what's happening online. Let's be honest, you're all there to communicate with each other, not to sit with your head in your phone.

If you feel strongly about banning your friends from using their phones at the table, ask them to put their phones in a bowl at the start of the night and tell them they'll get them back when they leave. You may have to make an exception if your friends are avid Instagrammers and need to photograph every meal they consume.

The perfect guest

+ Always RSVP. Don't turn up on the day if you haven't indicated that you are coming; your host may not have catered for you.
+ Don't bring a guest unless you ask first. Again, your host will be catering for each person, so they'll need to know exact numbers in advance. The same goes for children; check in advance if it is a child/baby-friendly event.
+ Don't be late. Arriving more than fifteen minutes' late to an event is disrespectful to your party host, who may be counting down the minutes for when to serve hot food. If you are going to be late, send a message to let them know.
+ We all have stressful days, and it's important you don't bring your bad mood with you to the party. Put that aside and enter the house with a happy disposition and some excellent banter at the ready.
+ If there is a dress code, stick to it. You don't want to be the odd one out. If you are unsure of the dress code, ask in advance.
+ Always offer to help the host with any food preparation or table setting. Likewise, offer to clear the table, or just stand up and start doing it. That way your host can't refuse and will probably be very thankful for the help.
+ Consider toasting the host as dinner is served.
+ A thank you note the next day is always appreciated to acknowledge the hard work your host has gone to. Failing that, send them a thank you email or text.

Celebration

'A thank you note the next day is always appreciated to acknowledge the hard work your host has gone to.'

Gift
ideas

Most hosts will tell you not to bring anything, but it's always a nice touch to show your appreciation for their efforts – and expense too, if they've catered a full sit-down meal with matching wines. A small gift is all that's needed.

+ box of chocolates
+ posey of flowers
+ champagne

+ small potted plant
+ coffee-table book
+ board game

The perfect neighbour

+ Make sure your party etiquette extends to your neighbours, too. If you think your party may end up being a little raucous, tell your neighbours that you're planning on entertaining and that you'll do your best to keep the noise down.
+ If you don't know your neighbours very well then pop a friendly note in their letterbox advising them of the date and time of the party, noting that the music will be turned down at midnight. They may be less likely to make a complaint with forewarning.
+ When the party has ended, politely ask your guests to keep the noise down as they leave. This is especially important if you live in an apartment complex.
+ It's probably not a good idea to take the empty wine and beer bottles to the bin before 9 am the next day, to avoid waking the neighbours with the noisy sound of clanging glass.

'If you don't know your neighbours very well then pop a friendly note in their letterbox.'

Tidy routines

One of the most important things about having people over – whether planned or impromptu – is making sure that your house is clean and organised. You will also find that a tidy house makes you feel more relaxed, even when it's just you at home. Keeping your house tidy can be a struggle at times, especially if you live with other people, but you can utilise some routines to keep things a little less chaotic. It will mean a lot less work whenever you do have people over!

Daily routine

+ Make the bed – it doesn't have to be complicated. Just pulling the doona over the sheets and popping a few cushions on top is all you need to commit to.
+ Don't leave clothes lying around. Laundry baskets hide all manner of sins until laundry day.
+ Wash the dishes or stack the dishwasher, give the kitchen a quick sweep, and wipe down the kitchen benches before bed each night. It's much nicer waking up to a tidy kitchen rather than last night's dinner plates piled up in the sink.

'A tidy house makes you more relaxed, even when it's just you at home.'

Weekly routine

+ General tidy up: dust, vacuum and sweep.
+ Clean the bath, shower and toilets. Spray and wipe down the bathroom sinks and mirrors.
+ Spray and wipe over the kitchen benchtops and wipe over the oven and microwave.
+ Mop the kitchen and bathroom floors.
+ Fluff the sofa cushions up.
+ Clear the mail and any other clutter from the hall table.
+ Make an effort to put all the laundry away.

If you can afford a cleaner, having someone come in weekly or fortnightly can make a huge difference to your overall happiness. If living with friends, this is something you could realistically afford as you can split the cost – plus it will save a lot of arguments over who cleans what and when.

And if people do pop around unexpectedly?

Instead of flying through the house like a tornado, picking up wine glasses and dirty clothes as you go, try these simple tricks – you'll look like you live in a pristine palace all the time.

+ Close the doors to any bedrooms in disarray.
+ Quickly pull the doona over any beds that are on display.
+ Do a quick lap around the bathroom: clean the toilet, wipe down the sink and vanity, and replace the hand towel if needed.
+ Throw any dirty dishes into the dishwasher or sink.
+ Wipe down the kitchen bench and put out a new tea towel (dish towel).
+ Catch your breath, brush your hair and light a candle. They'll never know ...

Decorate

1/2

Decorate

Connecting with friends and loved ones isn't the only important element when entertaining. Setting the table, going crazy with decorations and spreading the cheer throughout your home is all part of the fun. It shows your guests that you care about them, that you've gone to some effort to set the right mood.

SETTING THE SCENE

You can have a lot of fun with all kinds of decorations for your celebration, but there are a few basics that you'll likely always want to use. It's a good idea to buy some of these items in bulk and store them in your dining room buffet or kitchen cupboard (it helps to have a designated box for them), so you don't have to take a trip to the shops every time you have a party.

+ **Balloons:** These come in all sorts of shapes, colours and sizes. Hang them over the table, at the front door, in the entryway or just dotted around the room.
+ **Confetti:** Confetti is always a fun party element for scattering across the table. Mind you, it's only for those who don't mind the clean up afterwards.
+ **Tissue paper honeycomb balls:** These work well when hung above your table or in clusters with balloons.
+ **Streamers:** The ultimate party accessory. Hang them across the room or above the table.
+ **Festoon lights:** Ideal for outdoor spaces, these pretty little lights will add a nice glow to your outdoor space.
+ **Boxes:** Upturned timber boxes make great tables for nibbles or desserts, and creating different levels of height adds visual interest to your table.
+ **Tablecloths:** These add colour to the space or can tie in with the party theme.

Tip

Gather a few little props that tie in with the party theme and place them around the house. House them neatly on boards or trays on the table so you can place food platters around them.

Place
cards

Are you hosting a dinner party that requires people to take specific seats at the table? Get creative with place cards to signal to guests where they should sit.

Some place card ideas

+ pretty stationery paper with calligraphy writing
+ Christmas ornament with a name tag tied around it
+ paper flag with the guest's name written on it
+ pine cone with a name tag attached
+ name tag tied with string around a napkin

FLOWERS

A trip to the flower market is one of my favourite elements of party planning. No party is complete without some pretty posies adorning the table. They add texture, colour and beauty to the room, brighten up bathroom benchtops and greet your guests with their happy faces at your entryway. Don't reserve them just for parties, though – flowers at any time can instantly lift a room, and often your mood, too.

Flower markets

Want to nab some flowers at bargain prices? Wholesale flower markets are usually open to the general public, although be warned: it's not a stroll through the fields – it's a hyper and buzzing atmosphere! But you'll enjoy wandering around all the stalls and you'll get to see such an amazing array of flowers that you don't see in many florists. Here is your guide to navigating the flower markets.

Arrive early

The early bird gets the best worms ... Flower markets typically open at 5 am – this is the time when most florists arrive because they're there to get the best quality to sell in their store over the next few days. Follow their lead! Because the markets start so early, the good stuff is usually gone by 9 am, although some vendors still hang around until 11 am. Check the opening hours and days of the markets before you go, as many only open every second day.

Cash is king

If you're buying bulk, then pay cash as you're more likely to get a discount, and not all vendors offer credit card facilities. Some markets charge an entry fee, so make sure you have cash ready when you drive in the gates.

Storage tubs

If you're planning to buy more than a few bunches (remember, you're getting up before dawn, so you might as well make it worth your while), you'll need something to carry the flowers in. Buckets and little trolleys are a great help.

Supplies

You can buy more than just beautiful blooms at the markets. There are supply stores selling ribbon, tissue paper, scissors for every use you can imagine, pruning shears, oasis (florist) foam, vases, floral wire and so much more.

Fresh is best

If you're buying for an event a few days away, look for buds that are still tightly closed. This is especially important if the weather is warm, as the buds will open up in the heat. Often some of the older stock is sold off cheaper; if the petals are still okay and the stems aren't slimy then they will be perfectly fine to use on the day.

Don't have time for a trip to the flower markets?

+ Visit your nearest florist. You'll be paying more than the flower markets, but you'll still get excellent quality flowers, and hopefully they'll even arrange them for you.
+ Stop at the supermarket or your local petrol station and pick up a few bunches of pre-wrapped flowers. Once you get home, you'll need to call on your creative talents to transform them from supermarket flowers to sophisticated posies. Unwrap them, remove the excess leaves and trim the stems before arranging them into smaller vases, which you can place around the house.
+ If you're lucky enough to have a garden, a few pretty stems or a bunch of leaves from a camellia or olive tree can look stunning in a vase.

How to get the most from your flowers

Never just dump a bunch of flowers into water; that is a crime of the third degree. Next time you're given a beautiful bunch of florals, follow these steps to get the most out of them.

+ Clean the vase with soapy water and rinse well, then fill the vase with lukewarm water.
+ Unwrap the flowers from all plastic or paper wrapping. Carefully remove the rubber band around the stems, as well as any other protective casing.
+ Cut all the stems on a 45-degree angle, trimming them to a length suitable for the flower head to sit just above the top of the vase. Trimming the stems helps the flowers absorb the fresh water better and keeps them alive for longer. When trimming flowers to fit into your vase, move the vase to the edge of the table you're working at. Hold the stems against the edge of the table, with the head of the flower at the top of the vase. This will help you work out what height to cut the stems so they sit perfectly in your vase, and saves you ending up with stems that are too long or too short. Note: if it's a thick stem (resembling a stick), you'll need to slice down the centre of the stem to allow the water to get through. Sometimes it's necessary to smash the stems a bit if they're stiff.
+ Remove any leaves that will be sitting under the water once the stems are in the vase. Leaving the leaves on turns the water murky much faster and shortens the life of the flowers (plus the water smells terrible). Use a rose stripper to get the leaves off quickly and easily (and without stabbing yourself on the thorns if you're dealing with roses).
+ Pop your pretty stems into the vase and find a happy home for them to sit, away from direct sunlight or air-conditioning vents.
+ To keep the flowers fresh, change the water daily or every second day. Trim the stems every few days if needed, to revive them and keep the flowers alive a little longer, and remove any dying flowers from the bunch.

The anatomy of a bouquet

It can be hard to arrange flowers in a vase and make them look as nice as a florist can. Follow this rule of three to create your own perfect posies.

+ Start with a hero bloom. These are the biggest and most beautiful stems in the bunch – typically a flower such as a peony, rose, dahlia or hydrangea. Hold the stem of your hero bloom in your hand at a 45-degree angle.
+ Now, working with one bloom at a time, start to add secondary blooms around the hero bloom. Good secondary stems are ranunculus, poppies, sweet pea, lisianthus and spray roses. They aren't always bright and colourful; secondary stems are often white or green to blend in with the bunch.
+ After you've added three or four secondary blooms, add in some foliage. Adding foliage to your flowers bulks out the bouquet and adds a charming 'undone and loose' touch. Your existing flowers' stems and leaves will dictate which tone of foliage to opt for – it can look a little off if you put light-green flower stems with dark-green foliage.

Keep going in this manner, working around the central bloom in a diagonal motion until you can't hold any more in one hand. Then trim the stems and place into a vase.

Celebration — Decorate

Tip

It helps to hold the bouquet below your waist and look down onto it to see if everything is evenly spaced. You can always pick blooms out that aren't sitting quite right or rework the placement.

Guide to vases

You can fashion a vase out of just about anything, but choosing the right vase will make or break your bouquet (literally). Choose wisely for the types of flowers you are arranging, making sure that the height or weight of the vessel will support the blooms. A short, open vase won't be able to keep taller, heavy stems upright and may tip over. Choose the vase to suit the occasion as well. Crystal-cut vases are an elegant option for a fancy formal dinner, whereas a ceramic jug is better suited to a more casual afternoon picnic table.

+ **Cubed vase:** This is a great option for arranging flowers of the same variety. Using flowers in one variety and colour has a lot of impact when done well. Cut the stems to the length of the vase so that your flowers sit just at the top of the vase.
+ **Column vase:** For the flowers to have an impact in a tall vase, you'll need to choose flowers with long stems. Cherry blossoms, foxglove, roses and magnolias are good options.
+ **Flared vase:** It helps to arrange the posy in your hand first so that the arrangement sits neatly out of the vase like a bouquet. This type of vase is good for tulips, as it allows them to flop artfully out of the vase.
+ **Bud vases:** This type of vase is a great option if your bouquet is reaching the end of its life or you only have garden flowers available to arrange. Trim the stems just below the buds and pop them into the vases. These look great scattered along a dinner table when serving share platters.
+ **Fishbowl vase:** Short and squat in stature, these make great dining table vases. They can't house very tall flowers, so you can still have a conversation with the person opposite you without having to navigate through a jungle.
+ **Cut glass or crystal:** These are a little old fashioned but still a classic staple in any home. They suit traditional flowers such as roses or peonies.
+ **Old pitchers or jugs:** These give an old-worldy charm or cottage feel. They suit country garden florals such as lavender, freesias and hydrangeas.

+ Jars: You don't have to spend big to create an impact. Fill jars left over from jam, pasta, condiments or even candles with pretty blooms and display them en masse down the length of your dining table.

Tip

If you aren't one for daily maintenance, opt for a vase in a solid colour rather than a glass one. The water in clear glass vases needs replacing daily, as it can quickly turn cloudy.

Reflexing
roses

If you're an avid Instagrammer, you will no doubt have seen the trend of reflexing single-stem roses. What is reflexing, you say? Glad you asked. Here's a step-by-step guide to get those big, 'Alice in Wonderland' roses at home.

+ Buy a bunch of single-stem roses (the bigger the bud the better). Note that two- or three-day-old roses are better for reflexing than freshly picked roses.
+ Remove any brown or older rose petals.
+ Gently fold the outer petals back on themselves so that the rose appears to open right up.
+ Do this for about two or three layers of petals.
+ Voilà! You've got yourself a big, fat, juicy-looking rose! Arrange a bunch of them in a pretty vase or pop them in bud vases and dot them around the house.

Toolkit

If you're serious about wrangling bunches of blooms, you might want to consider investing in a few basics for your floristry tool belt.

+ **Apron:** Flower arranging is messy business, so wear an apron to keep your clothes out of harm's way. An apron with pockets is handy for storing your tools while you work.
+ **Gloves:** These are especially useful if you are handling roses or anything with thorns.
+ **Buckets:** Vital for keeping your blooms hydrated while you play around with different configurations in your vases. Use them also as a rubbish bin to collect rejected stems and leaves.
+ **Floral knife:** Use this for slicing rose thorns off stems and cutting any stubborn stems that your secateurs can't break through.
+ **Floral scissors:** These usually come with yellow handles so you can distinguish them from your everyday scissors. They are fairly sturdy, so they can cut through thick stems.
+ **Ribbon scissors:** Use these for cutting ribbon only. If you use them to trim stems or cut paper you will blunt them, and you'll only end up fraying your ribbons when you go to cut them.
+ **Pliers:** Used to control thicker wire.
+ **Pruning shears or secateurs:** To cut through thicker stems or sticks.
+ **Rose strippers:** Swiftly strip the leaves off roses using these magical creations, while avoiding any serious thorn injuries.
+ **Floral tape:** Used to camouflage stems and protect the scalp from the sharp floral wire when making floral headpieces or hair combs. The tape is sticky and stretchy, so it's pliable as you work.
+ **Floral wire:** Available in various thicknesses, this is used for wiring individual stems in headpieces, bouquets, buttonholes and more.
+ **Twine:** Holds the bunch of flowers in place before you tie them with ribbon.
+ **Oasis (florist) foam:** Available in a huge range of shapes and sizes, oasis foam is used instead of a vase. Pre-soak the foam in water and then stab the stems into the damp foam. The foam is also useful when placed in large vases (that aren't clear glass) to keep stems standing up straight.
+ **Water spritzer:** Especially useful on hot days for fragile petals.

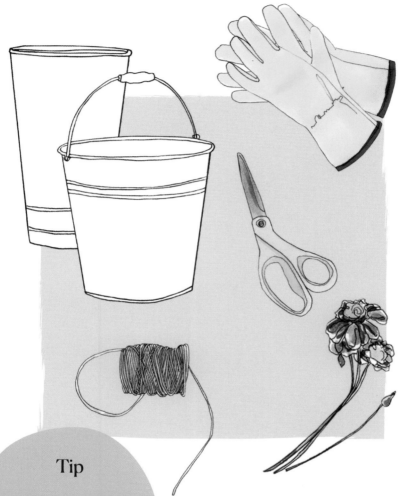

Tip

Elastic bands and safety pins have a million uses – including in flower bouquets. Use an elastic to secure your bouquets, and safety pins to secure ribbon or to attach flowers to buttonholes or napkins.

Light
it up

Lighting is an especially important part of the look of any evening event. Make sure you can control the light levels to add some mood lighting to the room. When everyone sits down to eat, turn off any bright overhead lights and light some candles instead.

'Lighting is an especially important part of the look of any evening event.'

Table
centrepieces

A fun way to get your table in the party mood is to style up a centrepiece in the theme of your celebration. If you are hosting an event that doesn't require sitting at the table, fill your table with platters, flowers and other styling elements and use it as the main focal point for the space. If your guests will be sitting down to eat, maybe opt for smaller decorative items – your centrepiece should look beautiful but still allow for elbow room and for conversations to happen across the table!

It seems a bit of a crime to leave your dining table completely void of any decorative accessories when it's not in use, so don't just save centrepieces for celebrations. Items for your centrepiece:

Items for your centrepiece

+ trays
+ candles
+ lanterns
+ hurricane lamps

+ cloches
+ terrariums
+ bowl of fruit
+ fresh flowers

+ clam shell
+ urns
+ candlesticks
+ potted orchid

Tip

Living things are always nicer on your table than things that will gather dust, but there are plenty of lovely faux flowers on the market that will do the trick as a year-round centrepiece.

Ideas for your centrepiece

+ Grouping items is a good way to fill the table and get a bit of wow factor happening. Flowers in vases of varying heights are a great option and don't necessarily cost a fortune to put together.
+ A tray of large pillar candles provides additional light and atmosphere for a party. The pillar candles will drip wax and look fab, but you'll need to ensure they're on a tray to prevent damaging the dining table.
+ If you are lucky enough to have good natural light, consider some of the many beautiful (and tough) succulents as a centrepiece that will look beautiful long after your guests leave. They can be bought already potted up or transplanted into an attractive vessel in keeping with your decor.
+ Use a table runner or tablecloth to add some texture or colour.

'It seems a bit of a crime to leave your dining table completely void of any decorative accessories when it's not in use, so don't just save centrepieces for celebrations.'

Eat + Drink

2/2

Eat + Drink

You've got the decorations under control, so now it's time to think about the food and drinks you're going to serve. For many this is possibly the most important consideration when it comes to entertaining. Sure, it's not the only reason why your friends are visiting, but the food you serve indicates the theme of the evening just as much as the decor, plus it's the central element that brings everyone around the table. It shows your guests that you've made an effort for them, that you are welcoming them into your home to share a delicious meal.

SETTING THE TABLE

Most of the parties you'll have at home will probably be casual barbecues or informal dinners where you serve yourself from grazing plates and share platters. Then there are times that might call for something more fancy – perhaps a formal occasion that requires the dreaded formal dining setting. But which fork does what? Which side does the knife go on? Does the water glass sit on the same side as the wine glass? Use these lists as your go-to guide:

Casual dining setting

Whether you're setting the table for a casual sit-down dinner, or piling the crockery and cutlery off to the side for everyone to help themselves, this is what you'll need:

+ water glass
+ wine glass (red or white)
+ dinner plate
+ dinner fork

+ dinner knife
+ dessert spoon
+ salt and pepper shakers
+ napkin

Formal dining setting

Thankfully you probably don't sit down to a formal dinner every night of the week – that would be an exhaustive set-up – but when you do, you might need:

+ water glass
+ wine glass (red and white)
+ champagne glass
+ butter plate
+ charger plate

+ dinner plate
+ salad plate
+ bread plate
+ salad fork
+ dinner fork
+ dessert fork
+ butter knife
+ salad knife
+ dinner knife
+ dessert spoon
+ salt and pepper shakers
+ napkin

Tip

If you're using sterling silver cutlery, it's worth checking over the set the day before your event in case any of the pieces need polishing.

Celebration — *Eat + Drink*

Protecting your
furniture

If you've just spent a fortune on decorating your new home and you're opening it up to guests for the first time, make sure you protect any pieces of furniture you'd hate to have food or drinks spilled on. Consider putting anything really precious in another room to keep it safe.

Use placemats and tablecloths to protect your dining table from chips and scratches, especially if your table is glass (it will also help reduce the noise of cutlery banging on the glass top). If you have wooden side tables or coffee tables, provide coasters for your guests, to avoid nasty water rings on the timber.

THE ART OF CHEESEBOARDS

To keep a hungry crowd happy, you can't beat a cheeseboard – and you don't need to do any cooking! Cheeseboards make a great starter and they're also perfect at the end of a meal, or you can go all out and make the ultimate cheeseboard to serve as a main. Putting together the perfect cheeseboard is a bit like creating a work of art, and presentation is everything! Never under any circumstances should any items be served in their original packaging unless said packaging is very pretty. All items should be re-homed into tiny ceramic bowls or dishes.

Basic elements

+ large wooden breadboard (or place two together)
+ baking paper (stops cheese sticking to the board, making it easier to clean up afterwards)
+ variety of cheese knives
+ small bowls for dips
+ small bowl for olive pits
+ herbs for decoration
+ small vases of flowers dotted around the board
+ candles
+ serving plates
+ napkins

Tip

Do your guests have any dietary preferences, food intolerances or allergies? You don't want to serve up your magnificent creation only to discover half your guests are vegan, lactose-intolerant or allergic to nuts.

What to serve

Here's what you'll need for the perfect cheeseboard as an appetiser for eight to ten people:

+ **Cheese:** Don't crowd your platter with every fancy *fromage* under the sun. You want a mixture of hard and soft cheeses that vary in size, shape and colour to make the cheeseboard more visually appealing – perhaps two hard and two soft. (Turn to the next page for a quick guide to cheeses.)
+ **Texture:** Nuts such as walnuts, almonds, pine nuts and peanuts are great for texture. A few handfuls should do.
+ **Freshness:** Fruit such as figs, berries, sliced pear or apple add freshness – red or green grapes served on their vine add a creative touch.
+ **Sweetness:** This comes from quince paste or dried fruit like apricots, figs, bananas, prunes, sultanas (golden raisins), raisins and cranberries. Chocolates are always a winner as well!
+ **Saltiness:** Italian meat cuts make a great addition to your cheeseboard – think thinly sliced prosciutto, salami and sopressa. Otherwise a small bowl of stuffed bell peppers or green or black olives add a nice saltiness.
+ **Dips:** A selection of three dips brings some new flavours to your cheeseboard – try eggplant (aubergine), hummus, salmon and dill, grilled capsicum (pepper), guacamole, salsa, spinach, tzatziki, French onion, olive or taramosalata.
+ **Crackers and bread:** Make sure you have a mix of wheat-based and gluten-free crackers, along with slices of sourdough or baguette. I'd suggest three types of crackers and one or two types of bread.

Tip

When you're arranging the different elements on the cheeseboard, save the nuts until last. These can be scattered across the board to strategically fill any holes or gaps.

Cheese guide

There's a whole world of cheeses out there (over 1800, in fact), so don't be afraid to try something new. But if you don't know your pecorino from your parmesan, use the guide below to avoid any bamboozlement at the deli counter.

Hard cheeses

+ **Cheddar:** One of the most popular of the hard cheeses, cheddar is creamy and sharp all in one.
+ **Emmental:** Distinguished by its large holes, this is a mild cheese made from cow's milk.
+ **Gouda:** This is a semi-hard, creamy, full-flavoured cheese with a nutty aftertaste.
+ **Gruyère:** A hard cheese originating in Switzerland with a fruity, nutty flavour.
+ **Halloumi:** Nicknamed the squeaky cheese, this is a semi-hard, salty cheese made from a mixture of goat's and sheep's milk, although some now contain cow's milk.
+ **Manchego:** Pale in colour and made from sheep's milk, this semi-hard cheese has a fruity, nutty flavour.
+ **Pecorino:** From the word *pecora*, meaning sheep in Italian, pecorino is a group of cheeses made from sheep's milk. Look for pecorino sardo, which has a salty, slightly fruity tang, or pecorino romano.

'There's a whole world of cheeses out there, so don't be afraid to try something new.'

Soft cheeses

+ **Bocconcini:** Small round balls of mozzarella cheese, often served with basil and tomatoes.
+ **Brie:** This is a great all-round cheese with a creamy yet slightly tangy flavour.
+ **Burrata:** A fresh, soft, milky-textured cheese made from mozzarella and cream. Serve it as a large ball ready to be sliced into.
+ **Camembert:** A soft and tangy cheese.
+ **D'Affinois:** A French cheese with a very creamy texture. Similar to brie but with a stronger flavour.
+ **Feta:** Super crumbly in texture with a tangy and salty taste. Use it as a topping for all sorts of dishes, especially Greek and Italian.
+ **Goat's cheese:** This cheese has a very strong flavour with a similar texture to feta.
+ **Gorgonzola:** A crumbly and firm blue cheese made from cow's milk.
+ **Havarti:** A semi-soft cheese from Denmark, pale in colour with a buttery and sweet flavour.
+ **Jarlsberg:** Originating from Norway, this is a pale-yellow cheese with a buttery taste, and dotted with large round holes throughout.
+ **Mozzarella:** Originating from Italy and traditionally made using buffalo milk (though made from cow's milk nowadays), this cheese has a bouncy consistency and a milky flavour.
+ **Stilton:** A blue cheese from Britain, this is very strong in flavour, yet creamy and crumbly all in one.

Celebration — Eat + Drink

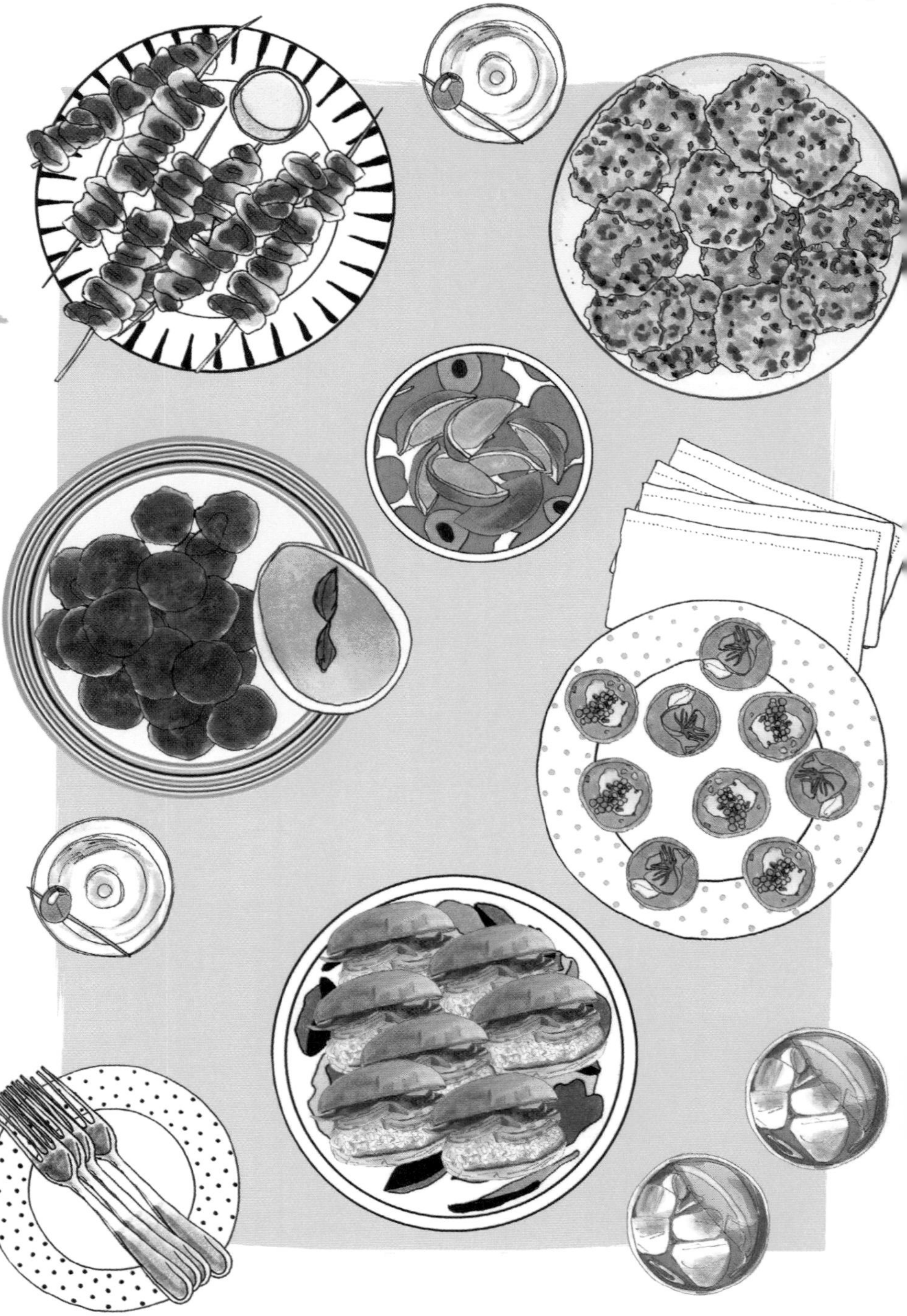

Canapés
101

If your guests are expected to be at your event for two or three hours, it would be wise to have at least four to six small bites on offer prior to the main meal. If you are only serving canapés, allow for twelve canapés per person. Some ideas include:

+ blinis
+ mini quiches
+ arancini balls
+ croquettes
+ corn fritters

+ smoked salmon pâté
+ spicy chicken skewers
+ cheese puffs
+ mini beef meatballs
+ smoked salmon on rye

Tip

If you think you haven't catered enough, serve bread rolls or slices of bread with the meal as an extra filler.

Chicken and pistachio sandwiches

Serves 6
70 g (2½ oz) butter
12 slices wholemeal
   (whole-wheat) bread
260 g (9 oz/1½ cups) shredded
   barbecue chicken breast
   (skin removed)
1 celery stalk, finely sliced
65 g (2¼ oz/½ cup) finely
   chopped pistachio nuts
1½ tablespoons sour cream
2 tablespoons mayonnaise

Butter each slice of bread. Place all the remaining ingredients in a bowl and mix together gently. Season with salt and pepper if preferred. Spoon teaspoons of the mixture onto six slices of bread and spread out to cover the bread. Place the remaining bread slices on top.

Trim off the crusts and then cut each sandwich into three finger sandwiches.

Egg and caviar dip

Serves 4
6 eggs, hard-boiled and peeled
125 g (4½ oz/½ cup) butter,
   at room temperature
1 tablespoon finely chopped
   spring onions (scallions)
250 g (9 oz/1 cup) sour cream
2 tablespoons snipped chives
3 x 50 g (1¾ oz) jars red
   and black caviar

Put the eggs, butter and spring onions in a bowl, season with salt, then mash together with a fork. Transfer to a shallow serving dish and chill.

Before serving, spoon the sour cream over the top and spread it out to cover, top with the chives and decorate with red and black caviar in any pattern you like (perhaps a Christmas tree or a heart on Valentine's Day).

Chocolate mousse

Serves 4

250 g (9 oz) block dark
  chocolate, chopped
5 eggs, separated
50 g (1¾ oz) caster
  (superfine) sugar
1 teaspoon vanilla extract
200 g (7 oz) savoiardi
  (sponge finger) biscuits
60 g (2 oz/½ cup) raspberries
1 gold-leaf sheet

Put the chocolate in a saucepan over low heat and stir until melted. Add the egg yolks and stir to combine. In a clean, dry bowl, beat the egg whites and sugar until soft peaks form. Fold the whisked egg whites and vanilla into the melted chocolate mixture.

Line the base and side of a trifle bowl with the savoiardi biscuits, then pour the mousse into the bowl. Refrigerate for 30 minutes to set. Top with raspberries and decorate with flakes of gold leaf (use a small paintbrush to place the gold leaf on the raspberries).

Shirley's apricot biscuits

Makes about 25

170 g (6 oz) unsalted butter,
  at room temperature, plus
  extra for greasing
450 g (1 lb) caster
  (superfine) sugar
4 teaspoons apricot jam
225 g (8 oz/1¾ cups)
  self-raising flour

Preheat the oven to 180°C (350°F) and lightly grease two baking trays. Cream the butter and sugar in a bowl using an electric mixer until light and fluffy. Add the jam and then the flour and stir together until well combined.

Break off small pieces of dough and roll them into balls. Place on the trays (don't press down with a fork) and bake for 8–12 minutes, or until light golden. Leave on the trays to cool, then serve.

Lamb skewers

Serves 4
500 g (1 lb 2 oz) diced lamb
   leg steak
1 red capsicum (bell pepper),
   diced
2 zucchini (courgettes), diced
1 red onion, thickly sliced
olive oil cooking spray
juice of 2 lemons
3 garlic cloves, crushed
2 teaspoons dried mint

Alternately thread the diced lamb, capsicum, zucchini and onion onto kebab skewers. Spray the lamb skewers with olive oil spray. Combine the lemon juice, garlic and dried mint in a bowl and spread evenly over the skewers. Season with salt and pepper.

Preheat the barbecue to a medium–high heat for 10 minutes. Grill the skewers for 6–7 minutes, rotating the skewers every few minutes, or until cooked to your satisfaction.

Barbecued corn

Serves 4
4 corn cobs
80 g (2¾ oz) butter, softened
1 teaspoon paprika
olive oil cooking spray
sea salt
1 spring onion (scallion),
   finely chopped

Preheat the barbecue to a medium–high heat. Remove the husks from the corn cobs. Brush the corn with the butter, sprinkle with paprika and spray with olive oil spray. Sprinkle with sea salt.

Cook the corn, turning, for 5–6 minutes until the corn is cooked through (leave it to slightly char if you like). Sprinkle with spring onion before serving.

Potato salad

Serves 4
8 all-purpose potatoes, such
  as desiree, peeled and cut
  into large cubes
1–3 tablespoons olive oil
250 g (9 oz) middle-cut bacon
  rashers (slices), diced
4 garlic cloves, crushed
150 g (5½ oz) croutons
250 g (9 oz/1 cup) sour cream
250 g (9 oz/1 cup) plain yoghurt
250 g (9 oz/1 cup) mayonnaise
fresh dill sprigs, to garnish

Cook the potatoes in a large
saucepan of boiling water until
tender and just cooked through.
Drain and allow to cool, then
transfer to a large serving bowl.

Heat 1 tablespoon of the olive
oil in a frying pan over medium
heat and fry the bacon and garlic
until crisp. Add the croutons to
the bacon and garlic and fry for
a further 3 minutes, adding more
oil as needed (the croutons will
soak up a lot of oil).

Combine the sour cream,
yoghurt and mayonnaise in a
bowl. Stir the sour cream mixture
through the potatoes until well
coated. Sprinkle with the fried
bacon and croutons, then garnish
with a few dill sprigs.

Greek salad

Serves 4
6 roma (plum) tomatoes
2 Lebanese (short) cucumbers
1 red onion
1 red capsicum (bell pepper)
200 g (7 oz) feta
100 g (3½ oz) kalamata olives
2 teaspoons dried oregano
150 ml (5 fl oz) olive oil

Dice the tomatoes, cucumbers,
onion, capsicum and feta.
Combine all the diced ingredients
in a salad bowl with the olives.
Sprinkle with the oregano, then
drizzle with the olive oil and
gently toss to combine.

Bring a
plate

Informal events are a great opportunity to call in some favours and ask your guests to each bring a plate to your party. This not only makes your life as a host a little less stressful, but then people who are gluten-free or vegetarian can bring something along that suits them. Here are some tips to prevent catering mayhem when you've asked everyone to 'bring a plate'.

+ If you've got a few friends who can hardly boil water, suggest they bring some bread, a pre-made salad or dessert.
+ Let everyone know how many guests will be attending so they can cater correctly.
+ Ask your guests to choose between bringing something sweet or savoury and make a note of it. That way you won't be serving up one main dish and nine desserts.
+ So you don't end up with a bunch of different dishes that don't really go together, tell your friends if you've got a particular theme, say Italian food, or if you're just having a barbecue with salads and breads.
+ If things don't go to plan or you run out of food, it pays to have some frozen quiches on hand for emergencies.

THE ART OF BAR CARTS

A well-stocked bar cart is always ready for action! Bar carts are excellent if you have a little nook in your living or dining room that needs filling, and they are usually on wheels so you can easily manoeuvre them around the room, or onto the balcony or into the backyard if you're having an outdoor party.

If you don't have space for a trolley, you can improvise. Place a large tray on your dining sideboard or even the TV unit in your living space and arrange a smaller selection of bar essentials on the tray. If you have lots of space, why not go all out by designating a special area of your dining room to your bar needs. If you have the option, think about installing a sink so you can clean up as you go when making your cocktails.

To get your bar cart up to scratch before hosting your next champagne breakfast or cocktail party, here's what you'll need.

+ **Muddler:** To mash up cocktail ingredients.
+ **Cocktail shaker:** To shake the cocktail contents together.
+ **Strainer:** Strains the cocktail into the cocktail glass.
+ **Corkscrew:** Many wine bottles are sealed with a screw cap these days, particularly Australian wines, but you'll still need a corkscrew.
+ **Ice bucket:** To chill your champagne and wine.
+ **Ice cubes:** For your ice bucket.
+ **Cocktail umbrellas:** For decoration.
+ **Peeler:** To peel any citrus rind for your cocktails.
+ **Pourer:** To aid your wine pouring.
+ **Bottle opener:** To open any bottle tops.
+ **Stirring spoon:** Also known as a swizzle stick, these are used to swirl your cocktail ingredients around.
+ **Cocktail picks:** To skewer any cocktail garnishes.
+ **Jigger:** A shot glass for measuring liquor.
+ **Punch bowl:** To serve your cocktail punch in.
+ **Drinks tray:** To serve your drinks to guests.

Mix up the liquor bottle sizes and shapes to keep the bar cart interesting. A mix of white spirits and darker spirits ensures you are catering to all guests' tastes, too. And keep a good stock of mixers and garnishes.

+ gin
+ vodka
+ tequila
+ scotch
+ whisky
+ vermouth
+ cognac
+ brandy
+ rum
+ port
+ sherry

+ tonic water
+ ginger ale
+ sparkling water
+ Angostura bitters

+ limes
+ lemons
+ sugar cubes
+ glacé cherries
+ olives

How much is too much?

You don't want to run out of wine halfway through your sit-down dinner party, nor do you want to be responsible for your guests' hangovers the next day. Use the guide below to cater sufficiently for your guests.

+ For wine, allow for one bottle between two people over a two-hour dinner.
+ For beer, allow two bottles per person in the first hour and one every hour after that.
+ Importantly, always ensure there are plenty of glasses and carafes of water on the table, and keep them topped up.

Tip

Make sure you're serving enough food with your alcohol, and that there is plenty of water or non-alcoholic drinks available for the designated drivers or those who don't drink.

Sparkling pink punch

Serves 4

115 g (4 oz/½ cup) caster (superfine) sugar
500 ml (17 fl oz/2 cups) soda water (club soda)
1 x 750 ml (25½ fl oz) bottle rosé wine
250 g (9 oz) strawberries
ice cubes, to serve

Put the sugar and 125 ml (4 fl oz/½ cup) of the soda water in a saucepan and bring to the boil, then reduce the heat and simmer for 2–3 minutes until the sugar has dissolved.

Pour the rosé into a large glass jug (pitcher). Slice three or four strawberries and add to the wine, then pour in the sugar syrup and the remaining soda water and stir to combine. Serve over ice and garnish with a whole strawberry.

Kiss the bride

Serves 6

1 x 750 ml (25½ fl oz) bottle chilled champagne
180 ml (6 fl oz) Cognac
6 sugar cubes
250 g (9 oz) strawberries, sliced

Fill each glass with champagne, not quite to the top. Add a nip (30 ml/1 fl oz) of Cognac, a sugar cube and a few slices of strawberry to each glass.

White wine sangria

Serves 4

60 ml (2 fl oz/¼ cup) brandy
1 x 750 ml (25½ fl oz) bottle
  dry white wine
500 ml (17 fl oz/2 cups)
  apple juice
2 tablespoons caster
  (superfine) sugar
1 peach, sliced
2 mandarins, peeled and diced
1 litre (34 fl oz/4 cups) soda water
  (club soda)
250 g (9 oz) strawberries, sliced

Combine the brandy, wine, apple juice and sugar in a large glass jug (pitcher). Stir until the sugar dissolves. Add the peach and mandarin, stir, then pour in the soda water. Refrigerate for 1 hour. Just before serving, add the strawberries and stir to combine.

Celebration — Eat + Drink

Pimm's jug

Serves 4

160 ml (5½ fl oz) Pimm's
250 g (9 oz) strawberries, sliced
125 g (4½ oz) blueberries
1 orange, rind sliced into
  thick strips
½ cucumber, peeled and sliced
200 ml (7 fl oz) ginger ale
1 handful of mint leaves
ice cubes, to serve

Pour the Pimm's into a tall jug (pitcher). Add the strawberries, blueberries, strips of orange rind and cucumber slices. Top with the ginger ale. Muddle the mint and add to the jug – use the swizzle stick to combine all the ingredients. Add ice and serve.

Entertaining
outside

Taking the party outside means you will be entertaining differently to the way you would indoors. Now you have to think about how things such as the weather, temperature and insects may affect the comfort of your guests.

Decor

Pick a theme that works with the outdoors (put the glitter gun away!). Some themes to consider are tropical island, camping, Mexican fiesta, garden tea party and pool party.

Outdoor parties tend to be brighter and more colourful than indoor parties. Think about matching some of the colours in your outdoor furniture and soft furnishings with your party decor. You can add pops of colour with items such as tablecloths, placemats, napkins, plates and cutlery, piñatas, streamers, honeycomb balls and balloons.

Food

It brings a bit more excitement to the space if the theme runs from the decor through to the food you're serving. If it's a picnic party, your choice of food and method of serving will be different to the way you'd serve the same dishes inside. Finger food works well here, as do platters, so everyone can help themselves. One thing to be mindful of when eating outside is insects and bugs – keep food covered with netting, beeswax food wrapping or mesh food covers.

Lighting

Once the sun sets you'll need a lighting plan to keep the party going. Festoon lights or fairy lights hung from the ceiling or patio rafters give off a romantic vibe. Candles are a lovely touch in the evenings. Consider using citronella candles to keep bugs at bay.

Furniture

Unless you are hosting a picnic you'll need to make sure you've got enough seating so your guests aren't standing up for the entire event. If you don't have a suitable outdoor setting, you may need to hire some chairs and tables. A trestle table covered with a white linen tablecloth makes a great outdoor dining table option, or use it as the servery. If you are investing in a new outdoor dining table, look into extendable options so that you can accommodate a larger group if needed. You can keep the overflow chairs inside or in the garage when not in use.

Weather

The weather plays a huge part in the success of the event. If it's cold, how do you keep everyone warm? Do you need to hire some outdoor heaters or perhaps buy a brazier or fire pit (perfect for toasting marshmallows, too)? If it's hot, perhaps you need to erect some shade cloth or large umbrellas. Windy weather can also affect comfort levels. Think about tying tablecloth weights to the corners of the fabric to keep the tablecloth down and platters of food on the table.

Tip

Put out a basket of essentials to keep your guests comfortable throughout the day or evening. Include insect repellant, bandaids, sunscreen and hats if it's summer or a few scarves and throw rugs if it's winter.

Just like last time, this book was not a solo endeavour ...

To the team at Hardie Grant, once again you have come to the party big time and brought this book to life in a way I couldn't have even imagined. Thank you to Jane Willson for trusting me with dreaming up another concept and pulling together a fabulous team to make it happen – particular thanks must go to Emily Hart, Lucy Sykes-Thompson, Kim Rowney and illustrator Juliet Sulejmani.

To Mum and Dad, I owe a lot of what I've learned about decorating and creating a home to both of you. Thank you for showing the three of us from such a young age what a home is meant to look and feel like. To my brothers, Luke and Alexander, perhaps one day you'll both see the benefits of keeping a tidy house (and making your beds). I'll be ready and waiting with this book when that day comes!

Thank you to my clients who allow me to put the decorating skills I've written about in this book into practice. If it wasn't for you opening the doors to your homes and trusting me with the outcome I wouldn't be half the decorator I am today.

To my friends, thank you for sitting so patiently at my parties while cheeseboards were served, photographed at a million different angles and Instagrammed before you were allowed to eat. All those years of cheeseboard practice has finally paid off.

Unlike decorating projects, which come with strict budgets and briefs, writing is quite a selfish and indulgent process as I'm free to write about what I like. So thank you to all of my readers: if it wasn't for your shared love of my books I wouldn't be able to indulge in my love of writing.

Acknowledgements

Acknowledgements

Emma Blomfield is a modern-day innovator.

Emma's work brings together her sophisticated design prowess, fresh vision and sharp business acumen. She uses her repertoire of styling, colour and furnishings to deliver simple decorating concepts that combine function and aesthetics.

Emma consults for a wide range of clientele in both event styling and residential interior design in Sydney. Her extensive portfolio is dotted with celebrity clients, and she regularly hosts workshops across Australia. She has been influential in demystifying an industry once considered niche and has brought innovation to interior decorating with the launch of online personal style consultations and education programs.

Emma's first book, *Home*, was published in 2017.

Published in 2019 by Hardie Grant Books, an imprint of Hardie Grant Publishing

Hardie Grant Books (Melbourne)
Building 1, 658 Church Street
Richmond, Victoria 3121

Hardie Grant Books (London)
5th & 6th Floors
52–54 Southwark Street
London SE1 1UN

hardiegrantbooks.com

A catalogue record for this
book is available from the
National Library of Australia

NATIONAL
LIBRARY
OF AUSTRALIA

Keeping House
ISBN 978 1 74379 486 9

10 9 8 7 6 5 4 3 2 1

Publishing Director: Jane Willson
Project Editor: Emily Hart
Editor: Kim Rowney
Design Manager: Jessica Lowe
Designer: Studio Polka
Production Manager: Todd Rechner

Colour reproduction by Splitting Image Colour Studio
Printed by Printed in China by Leo Paper Product. LTD